Table of contents

Message from Richard Cordray

Director of the CFPB

The Consumer Financial Protection Bureau (CFPB) is the Nation's only Federal agency whose sole focus is protecting consumers in the financial marketplace for products and services. When Congress created the Bureau through the Dodd-Frank Wall Street Reform and Consumer Protection Act of 2010, it provided the CFPB with a number of tools to fulfill our mission to make those markets work for Americans. Over the past fiscal year we have continued to achieve specific and tangible results for consumers whether they are applying for a mortgage, borrowing for college, choosing a credit card, or using any number of other consumer financial products.

During fiscal year 2014, CFPB enforcement actions resulted in almost $4 billion in penalties, redress and relief to consumers imposed against defendants who violated Federal consumer financial laws. For example, enforcement actions against several credit card companies provided relief of more than $1 billion to harmed consumers. The CFPB also ordered $2.6 billion in relief for consumers who were harmed by systemic misconduct by two mortgage servicers. Further, we assessed an additional $92.7 million in Civil Monetary Penalties to deter future occurrences of unfair, deceptive and abusive acts.

In Fall 2013, we issued a rule requiring easier-to-use mortgage disclosure forms that clearly lay out the terms of a mortgage for a homebuyer. The new forms integrate two overlapping forms that were each required by federal law for more than 30 years: the Truth in Lending Act form and the Real Estate Settlement Procedures Act form. Our new forms ensure that consumers have the information they need, when they need it and empower consumers to shop around for a mortgage, giving them greater control over their home-buying decisions.

During fiscal year 2014, we also issued a rule that allows the CFPB to supervise certain nonbank student loan servicers, making the Bureau the first federal agency to have oversight over this segment of the student loan market, which is the nation's second largest consumer debt market. The CFPB already oversees student loan servicing at large banks, but this new supervision of the nonbank loan servicers will provide the Bureau with visibility into nearly 50 million borrower accounts and will allow us to ensure that bank and nonbank student loan servicers are playing by the same rules.

The CFPB is committed to engaging with consumers and providing them with resources to help them navigate important decisions in their financial lives. For example, millions of Americans are managing money or property for a loved one who is unable to pay bills or make financial decisions on their own, which can be overwhelming work. In fiscal year 2014 we released four *Managing Someone Else's Money* guides to help these financial caregivers understand their duties, recognize scams and exploitation, and know where to get help when necessary. The Bureau also continues to build the AskCFPB interactive online tool, which provides consumers with clear, unbiased answers to their financial questions. The CFPB now has more than 1,000 plain-language entries on student loans, money transfers, and many other products and services, which consumers can search and browse by product categories and tags.

The CFPB continues to grow and mature as a Federal agency. In our first three years, we have grown from 58 employees at the beginning of fiscal year 2011 to 1443 employees at the end of fiscal year 2014. As we continue in our mission to make consumer financial markets work, we are committed to continued transparency into our performance and financial operations. As required by the Dodd-Frank Act, the CFPB prepared comparative financial statements for fiscal years 2014 and 2013. The Government Accountability Office (GAO) rendered an unmodified or "clean" audit opinion on our financial statements. GAO noted one (1) material weakness and cited no instances of noncompliance with laws and regulations.

I am very proud of our expert and enthusiastic staff and all of the great work they have accomplished over the past year, which is reflected in the assessment of our operations contained in this report. It attests to the persistent work of our colleagues who perform at the highest caliber and with a dedicated commitment to serve the public, protect consumers, support responsible businesses, and help safeguard the American economy.

Sincerely,

Richard Cordray

Richard Cordray

1. Management's Discussion and Analysis

1.1 The CFPB at a Glance: Overview of the Consumer Financial Protection Bureau

The Bureau of Consumer Financial Protection, known as the Consumer Financial Protection Bureau (CFPB or the Bureau), was established on July 21, 2010 under Title X of the Dodd-Frank Wall Street Reform and Consumer Protection Act Public Law No. 111-203 (Dodd-Frank Act). The CFPB was established as an independent bureau within the Federal Reserve System. The Bureau is an Executive agency as defined in Section 105 of Title 5, United States Code.

The Dodd-Frank Act authorizes the CFPB to exercise its authorities to ensure that, with respect to consumer financial products and services:

1. Consumers are provided with timely and understandable information to make responsible decisions about financial transactions;

2. Consumers are protected from unfair, deceptive, or abusive acts and practices and from discrimination;

3. Outdated, unnecessary, or unduly burdensome regulations are regularly identified and addressed in order to reduce unwarranted regulatory burdens;

4. Federal consumer financial law is enforced consistently in order to promote fair competition; and

5. Markets for consumer financial products and services operate transparently and efficiently to facilitate access and innovation.

Under the Dodd-Frank Act, on the designated transfer date, July 21, 2011, certain authorities and functions of several agencies relating to Federal consumer financial law transferred to the CFPB in order to accomplish the above objectives. These authorities were transferred from the Board of Governors of the Federal Reserve System (Board of Governors), Office of the Comptroller of the Currency (OCC), Office of Thrift Supervision (OTS), Federal Deposit Insurance Corporation (FDIC), National Credit Union Administration (NCUA), and the Department of Housing and Urban Development (HUD). In addition, Congress vested the Bureau with authority to enforce in certain circumstances the Federal Trade Commission's (FTC) Telemarketing Sales Rule and its rules under the FTC Act, although the FTC retains full authority over these rules. The Dodd-Frank Act also provided the CFPB with certain other Federal consumer financial regulatory authorities.

Organizational Structure

Under the Dodd-Frank Act, the Secretary of the Treasury was responsible for establishing the CFPB and performing certain functions of the Bureau until a Director of the CFPB was in place. The Bureau's day-to-day operations were managed by the Special Advisor to the Secretary of the Treasury for the Consumer Financial Protection Bureau until January 4, 2012, when President Obama nominated Richard Cordray to be the first Director of the CFPB. Subsequently, the U.S. Senate confirmed the nomination of Richard Cordray on July 16, 2013, and Director Cordray was sworn in as the first Senate-confirmed Director of the CFPB on July 17, 2013.

To accomplish its mission, the CFPB is organized into six primary divisions:

1. **Consumer Education and Engagement:** provides, through a variety of initiatives and methods, including offices on specific populations, information to consumers to empower them to make financial decisions that are best for them.

2. **Supervision, Enforcement and Fair Lending:** ensures compliance with Federal consumer financial laws by supervising market participants and bringing enforcement actions when appropriate.

3. **Research, Markets and Regulations:** conducts research to understand consumer financial markets and consumer behavior, evaluates whether there is a need for regulation, and determines the costs and benefits of potential or existing regulations.

4. **Legal Division:** ensures the Bureau's compliance with all applicable laws and provides advice to the Director and the Bureau's divisions.

5. **External Affairs:** manages the Bureau's relationships with external stakeholders and ensures that the Bureau maintains robust dialogue with interested stakeholders to promote understanding, transparency, and accountability.

6. **Operations:** builds and sustains the CFPB's operational infrastructure to support the entire organization and hears directly from consumers about challenges they face in the marketplaces through their complaints, questions, and feedback.

The CFPB workforce is spread across the country with its headquarters in Washington, D.C. and regional offices in Chicago, New York City, and San Francisco. The headquarters is temporarily spread across locations within Washington, D.C., utilizing space pursuant to interagency agreements with the Department of the Treasury (Treasury), the Office of the Comptroller of the Currency, the General Services Administration and the Federal Housing Finance Agency (FHFA). The workforce in the CFPB's regional offices is predominantly mobile and therefore relatively minimal office space is used in the regions.

Additional information on the organizational structure and responsibilities of the CFPB is available on CFPB's website at http://www.consumerfinance.gov/.

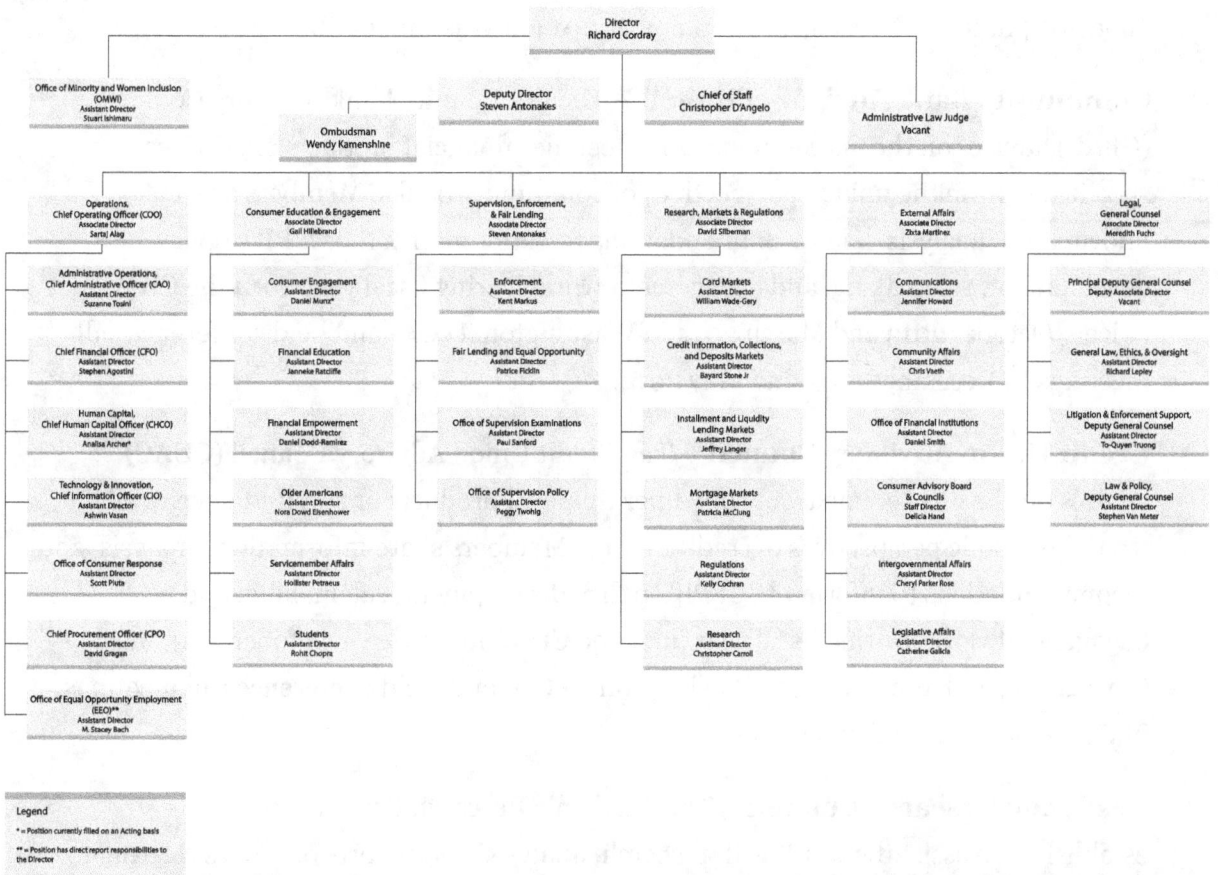

Advisory groups

The CFPB established four independent advisory bodies to provide consultation and advice to the Director on a range of issues within the CFPB's authority. Specifically, the CFPB has formally chartered the following advisory groups:

- **Consumer Advisory Board** – Through a public process, the Bureau invited external experts, industry representatives, consumers, community leaders, and advocates to nominate individuals to serve as members of this advisory group. The Consumer Advisory Board (CAB) is a group of experts on consumer protection, consumer financial products or services, community development, fair lending, civil rights, underserved communities, and communities that have been significantly impacted by higher-priced mortgage loans. They are a source of market intelligence and expertise, and they advise and consult on Federal consumer finance issues. The CAB informs the Director about emerging practices or trends in the consumer finance industry, and shares analysis and recommendations. Members are charged with identifying and assessing the impact of emerging products, practices, or services on consumers and other market participants. During fiscal year 2014 the CAB met three times – February 2014 in Washington D.C., June 2014 in Reno, Nevada, and September 2014 in Washington, DC.

- **Community Bank Advisory Council** – The Community Bank Advisory Council (CBAC) advises on the market impact of consumer financial products or services, specifically from the unique perspectives of community banks. Members share information, analysis, and recommendations to better inform the CFPB's policy development, rulemaking, and engagement work. During fiscal year 2014 the CBAC met twice – October 2013 and March 2014 in Washington, D.C. – and held conference call meetings in December 2013 and May 2014.

- **Credit Union Advisory Council** – The Credit Union Advisory Council (CUAC) advises on the market impact of consumer financial products or services, specifically from the unique perspectives of credit unions. Members share information, analysis, and recommendations to inform the CFPB's policy development, rulemaking, and engagement work. During fiscal year 2014 the CUAC met twice – October 2013 in Chicago, IL, and March 2014 in Washington, D.C. – and held conference call meetings in December 2013 and June 2014.

- **Academic Research Council** – The Academic Research Council (ARC) was established to assist the CFPB with research, analysis, and reports on topics relating to

CFPB's mission, including developments in markets for consumer financial products and services, consumer awareness, and consumer behavior. The Council is made up of scholars with relevant methodological and subject-matter expertise. The Council advises the CFPB on research methodologies, data collection, and analytic strategies, and provides feedback about research and strategic planning. During fiscal year 2014, the ARC held a meeting in April 2014 in Washington, D.C.

Growth of the CFPB

Since its inception, the CFPB has grown in the number of employees and the corresponding funding needed to carry out its duties and responsibilities. At the end of fiscal year 2014, the CFPB was still below the employment levels and funding it estimates it will need to achieve the mission and responsibilities mandated by Congress in the Dodd-Frank Act. The CFPB's growth to date has been relatively steady and consistent. The charts below provide a historical depiction of the growth for employees and funding levels.

FIGURE 1:   CFPB EMPLOYEES BY FISCAL YEAR

FIGURE 2: OFFICE PERCENTAGE OF TOTAL POSITIONS (AS OF SEPTEMBER 30, 2014)

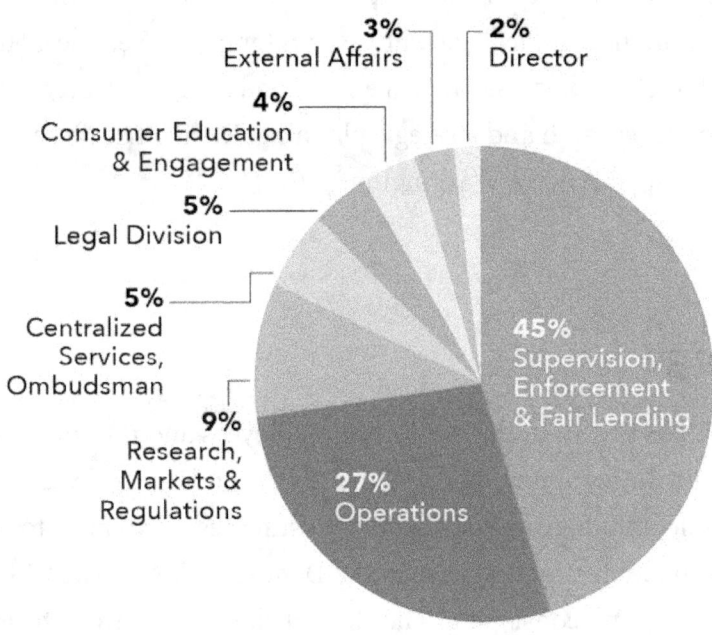

Within the Operations Division, displayed as 27% of total CFPB positions, the Office of Consumer Response comprises 11% of total CFPB positions, while all other Operations functions comprise 16%. All percentages provided above are rounded.

FIGURE 3: FISCAL YEAR TRANSFERS REQUESTED COMPARED TO THE FUNDING CAP ($ IN MILLIONS)

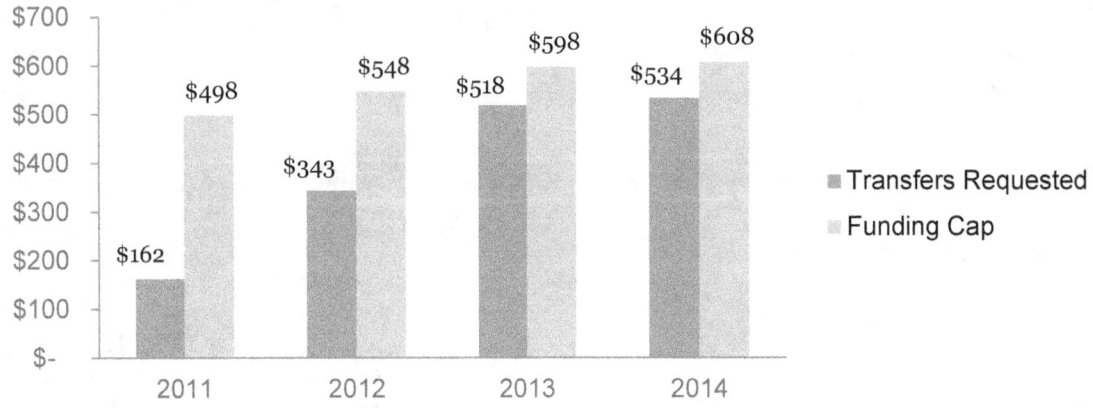

Additional information on how the CFPB is funded can be found in Section 1.5 Financial Analysis.

Mission, Vision, and Values

Our Mission

The CFPB is a 21st century agency that helps consumer financial markets work by making rules more effective, by consistently and fairly enforcing those rules, and by empowering consumers to take more control over their economic lives.

Our Vision

If we achieve our mission, then we will have encouraged the development of a consumer financial marketplace –

- Where customers can see prices and risks up front and where they can easily make product comparisons;

- In which no one can build a business model around unfair, deceptive, or abusive practices; and

- That works for American consumers, responsible providers, and the economy as a whole.

We will achieve our mission and vision through:

DATA-DRIVEN ANALYSIS

The CFPB is a data-driven agency. We take in data, manage it, store it, share it appropriately, and protect it from unauthorized access. Our aim is to use data purposefully, to analyze and distill data to enable informed decision-making in all internal and external functions.

INNOVATIVE USE OF TECHNOLOGY

Technology is core to the CFPB accomplishing its mission. This means developing and leveraging technology to enhance the CFPB's reach, impact, and effectiveness. We strive to be recognized as an innovative, 21st century agency whose approach to technology serves as a model within government.

VALUING THE BEST PEOPLE AND GREAT TEAMWORK

At the CFPB, we believe our people are our greatest asset. Therefore, we invest in world-class training and support in order to create an environment that encourages employees at all levels to tackle complex challenges. We also believe effective teamwork extends outside the walls of the CFPB. We seek input from and collaborate with consumers, industry, government entities, and other external stakeholders.

We aim to embody the following values in everything we do:

SERVICE

Our mission begins with service to the consumer and our country. We serve our colleagues by listening to one another and by sharing our collective knowledge and experience.

LEADERSHIP

Fostering leadership and collaboration at all levels is at the core of our success. We believe in investing in the growth of our colleagues and in creating an organization that is accountable to the American people.

INNOVATION

Our organization embraces new ideas and technology. We are focused on continuously improving, learning, and pushing ourselves to be great.

1.2 The CFPB performance and results

This section provides a summary of the CFPB's key performance outcomes as well as selected accomplishments that it has achieved this past fiscal year. This marks only the beginning of the Bureau's work on behalf of consumers and providers of financial products and services.

The CFPB developed and issued a strategic plan consistent with the Government Performance and Results Act (GPRA) that was compiled by the Office of the Chief Strategy Officer (see http://www.consumerfinance.gov/strategic-plan). The CFPB published its fiscal years 2013 to 2017 strategic plan in April 2013, which identifies four strategic goals and 28 associated performance measures. In order to meet the required due date of preparing and issuing this financial report not all performance measures could be included. However, a full Performance Report will be published in calendar year 2015, which will include the results of all 28 performance measures, along with an analysis of CFPB's efforts to achieve its performance goals. Results reported below for the selected measures contained in this report show that the CFPB has met or exceeded 12 of the 13 measures (92 percent).

Goal 1: Prevent financial harm to consumers while promoting good practices that benefit them

Prior to Congress enacting the Dodd-Frank Act, consumer financial protection had not been the primary focus of any one federal agency, and no agency could set the rules for the entire consumer financial market. The result was a system without sufficiently effective rules or consistent enforcement of the law. Consumer financial protection is the CFPB's singular focus.

PERFORMANCE GOAL

Complete consumer protection related rulemakings within nine months of receipt of final public comments.

TABLE 1: PERCENTAGE OF PROPOSED RULEMAKINGS, CONDUCTED SOLELY BY THE CFPB, FINALIZED OR OTHERWISE RESOLVED WITHIN NINE MONTHS OF THE DUE DATE FOR RECEIPT OF THE FINAL PUBLIC COMMENTS

	FY 2013	FY 2014
Target	75%	75%
Actual	78%	100%

In Fiscal Year 2014, the Bureau finalized and issued a number of rulemakings within the nine months of the closing of a final comment period. The Bureau made additional updates to its mortgage rules and issued an interim final rule amending provisions in Regulation Z and final rules issued by the Bureau earlier that year, which, among other things, required that consumers receive counseling before obtaining high-cost mortgages and that servicers provide periodic account statements and rate adjustment notices to mortgage borrowers, as well as engage in early intervention when borrowers become delinquent.

In November, 2013, the Bureau issued a final rule under Sections 1098 and 1100A of the Dodd-Frank Wall Street Reform and Consumer Protection Act (Dodd-Frank Act) along with forms that combined certain disclosures that consumers receive in connection with applying for and closing on a mortgage loan under the Truth in Lending Act (Regulation Z) and the Real Estate Settlement Procedures Act (Regulation X). The Bureau's final rule established new disclosure requirements and forms in Regulation Z for most closed-end consumer credit transactions secured by real property.

Also, the Bureau issued a final rule describing data instructions for lenders to use in complying with the requirement under the High-Cost Mortgage and Homeownership Counseling Amendments to the Truth in Lending Act (Regulation Z) and Homeownership Counseling Amendments to the Real Estate Settlement Procedures Act (RESPA Homeownership Counseling Amendments) Final Rule to provide a homeownership counseling list using data made available by the Bureau or Department of Housing and Urban Development (HUD).

In FY 2014, the Bureau amended Regulation E, which implements the Electronic Fund Transfer Act (EFTA), to provide new protections, including disclosure requirements, and error resolution and cancellation rights, to consumers who send remittance transfers to other consumers or businesses in a foreign country. The amendments implement statutory requirements set forth in the Dodd-Frank Act. The Bureau also made additional clarifying amendment and a technical correction to this final rule.

PERFORMANCE GOAL

Ensure that all rulemakings are informed by public outreach processes, such as Small Business Regulatory Enforcement Fairness Act (SBREFA) panels and consumer and industry roundtables.

TABLE 2: PERCENTAGE OF SIGNIFICANT CONSUMER PROTECTION RELATED, NOTICE-AND-COMMENT RULEMAKINGS INFORMED BY PUBLIC OUTREACH PROCESSES

	FY 2013	FY 2014
Target	100%	100%
Actual	100%	100%

During FY2014, CFPB rulemakings were informed by extensive public outreach efforts, including, roundtable events and outreach meetings with industry stakeholders and consumer advocates and as appropriate, Small Business Review Panel meetings with small business entities. The Bureau also received valuable input from members of its Consumer Advisory Board (CAB), Credit Union Advisory Council (CUAC), and Community Bank Advisory Council (CBAC).

Additionally, CFPB staff participated in numerous outreach meetings and external events to monitor implementation issues in connection with its mortgage and remittances rules, as well as interview testing with consumers around the country to help the Bureau develop and design the TILA-RESPA Integrated Disclosure rule, and posted the model disclosures on its website for public consideration and feedback.

PERFORMANCE GOAL

Successfully resolve the cases the CFPB files in court and administrative adjudicative proceedings whether by litigation, settlement, issuance of default judgment, or other means.

TABLE 3: PERCENTAGE OF ALL CASES FILED BY THE CFPB SUCCESSFULLY RESOLVED THROUGH LITIGATION, A SETTLEMENT, ISSUANCE OF DEFAULT JUDGMENT, OR OTHER MEANS

	FY 2013	FY 2014
Target	75%	100%
Actual	100%	100%

In FY 2014, the Bureau successfully resolved 40 public enforcement actions. These actions helped secure orders for almost $4 billion in penalties against defendants, redress and relief to more than 5.9 million consumers who fell victim to various violations of consumer financial protection laws. Of those 40 public enforcement actions, five related to fair lending, including HMDA data reporting violations as well as discrimination in mortgage pricing, auto loan pricing, and credit card debt collection. These fair lending actions resulted in orders for $284 million to address the harm of approximately 419,000 consumers.

Goal 2: Empower consumers to live better financial lives

The CFPB works to arm consumers with the knowledge, tools, and capabilities they need in order to make better-informed financial decisions by engaging them in the right moments of their financial lives, in moments when they are most receptive to seeking out and acting on assistance. To that end, the CFPB will develop and maintain a variety of tools, programs and initiatives that provide targeted, meaningful, and accessible assistance and information to consumers at the moment they need them.

PERFORMANCE GOAL

Decrease time between receiving and closing a complaint.

TABLE 4:   INTAKE CYCLE TIME

	FY 2013	FY 2014
Target	3 Days	3 Days
Actual	1 Day	1 Day

TABLE 5:   COMPANY CYCLE TIME

	FY 2013	FY 2014
Target	15 Days	15 Days
Actual	12 Days	12 Days

TABLE 6:   CONSUMER CYCLE TIME

	FY 2013	FY 2014
Target	30 Days	30 Days
Actual	4 Days	2 Days

TABLE 7:   INVESTIGATION CYCLE TIME

	FY 2013	FY 2014
Target	45 Days	45 Days
Actual	78 Days	56 Days

Complaint volume increased about 67 percent from 144,000 complaints in FY 2013 to 240,600 in FY 2014. In addition, Consumer Response added the ability to accept complaints about payday loans, prepaid cards, credit repair and debt settlement services, title and pawn loans and virtual currency during FY 2014. Consumer Response continued to refine its complaint handling processes and systems in FY 2014. Increasing efficiencies were achieved through improvements to product-specific complaint intake forms and automation where possible.

Actions were taken to address the increase complaint volume and complexity and to improve its overall complaint handling operation. Process refinements implemented in the investigations part of the complaint lifecycle as well as product-specific training in FY 2013 and FY 2014 continued to reduce the Investigations Cycle time in FY 2014.

PERFORMANCE GOAL: Facilitate the timely response to consumer complaints by companies.

TABLE 8:   PERCENTAGE OF COMPLAINTS ROUTED THROUGH THE DEDICATED COMPANY PORTAL

	FY 2013	FY 2014
Target	85 %	87 %
Actual	87 %	91 %

In FY 2014, the CFPB established company portal access and trained staff of approximately 700 companies to respond to complaints on the portal.

PERFORMANCE GOAL
Expand capacity to handle consumer complaints.

TABLE 9:   NUMBER OF CONSUMER COMPLAINTS HANDLED

	FY 2013	FY 2014
Target	125,000	200,000
Actual	144,000	240,600

In FY 2014, the Bureau expanded the products and services about which it accepts complaints beyond credit cards, mortgages, bank accounts and services, consumer loans, private student loan, money transfers, credit reporting, and debt collection complaints. In FY 2014, the CFPB began to accept complaints about payday loans, prepaid cards, credit repair and debt settlement services, title and pawn loans, and virtual currency. The Bureau plans to continue to expand its complaint handling to accept other products and services under its authority.

The Bureau also expanded its public Consumer Complaint Database, which was initially launched in June 2012 and populated with credit card complaints, to include complaints about additional products. In FY 2013, the Bureau added complaints about mortgages, bank account and services, private student loans, other consumer loan complaints, credit reporting, and money transfer complaints, as well as fields for sub-issue and state. In November 2013, debt collection complaints were added to the database. Payday complaints were added to the database in July 2014.

PERFORMANCE GOAL
Significantly increase targeted outreach activities and digital education materials in order to engage consumers at the right moment.

TABLE 10: TARGETED POPULATIONS OR ORGANIZATIONS DIRECTLY SERVING TARGETED POPULATIONS REACHED BY DIGITAL CONTENT, DECISION TOOLS, EDUCATIONAL MATERIALS AND RESOURCES

	FY 2013	FY 2014
Target	808,114	5,000,000
Actual	1,903,417	5,600,000

In FY 2014, the CFPB continued to serve consumers with just-in-time financial information through AskCFPB, an online database of consumers' common questions around financial products and services. The CFPB launched a major release of Paying for College, an online suite of information and tools for helping consumers to understand their after-graduation monthly debt payment before choosing a financial aid package. We also made investments in outreach that will maximize the awareness and value of our various products for consumers.

Goal 3: Inform the public, policy makers, and the CFPB's own policy-making with data-driven analysis of consumer finance markets and consumer behavior

Understanding how consumer financial markets work, the avenues for innovation in financial products and services, and the potential for risk to consumers is a core component of the CFPB's mission. The CFPB's aim is to ground all of its work – from writing rules and litigating enforcement actions to its outreach and financial literacy efforts – in the realities of the marketplace and the complexities of consumer behavior.

PERFORMANCE GOAL

Increase the number of reports produced about specific consumer financial products, markets, or regulations and on consumer decision-making.

TABLE 11: REPORTS PRODUCED ABOUT SPECIFIC CONSUMER FINANCIAL PRODUCTS, MARKETS, OR REGULATIONS AND ON CONSUMER DECISION-MAKING

	FY 2013	FY 2014
Target	5	5
Actual	4	8

Preparing reports is central to the Bureau's commitment to evidence-based policy-making. The Bureau issued eight prominent reports in FY 2014. These reports are intended to deepen the public's understanding of these issues and provide the Bureau and other policy makers with a stronger factual foundation on which to make policy judgments. In FY 2014, Bureau's Division of Research, Markets & Regulations (RMR) introduced a new "Data Point" report series. Data Point reports are prepared by the RMR Office of Research to provide an evidence-based perspective on consumer financial markets, consumer behavior, and regulations to inform the public discourse.

Goal 4: Advance the CFPB's performance by maximizing resource productivity and enhancing impact

In order to maximize the effectiveness of consumer protections established by Federal consumer financial law, the CFPB must acquire, maintain, support, and direct its resources in a way that enables it to operate efficiently, effectively, and transparently. This means developing, maintaining, and continuously improving the policies and controls in place to ensure the CFPB has the resources it needs and puts those resources to the best use possible.

A key mission of the CFPB is to make financial products and services more transparent in the consumer marketplace. The CFPB strives to achieve the same level of commitment to transparency in its own activities, while respecting consumer privacy and confidentiality. To accomplish this, the CFPB develops and implements mechanisms and provides channels to maintain an open, collaborative dialogue with the public.

PERFORMANCE GOAL

Release new datasets to the public, where legally permissible and appropriate, to allow for innovative uses of the data by individuals, non-profit entities, and businesses for the benefit of consumers.

TABLE 12: PROVISION OF DATA TO THE PUBLIC IN LEGALLY PERMISSIBLE AND APPROPRIATE INSTANCES

	FY 2013	FY 2014
Target	5 Data Sets	7 Data Sets
Actual	4 Data Sets	7 Data Sets

In FY 2014, the CFPB launched its public data platform for Home Mortgage Disclosure Act data, and updated the information with 2013 mortgage originations. This information will be available for use by industry advocates and consumers to intuitively search and work with the data and conduct analysis. The CFPB also released eRegs, a searchable tool for federal financial regulations. eRegs currently covers two major regulations for the financial industry, Reg Z and Reg E, and the Bureau is looking at potential opportunities for expansion. Also, in FY 2014, the CFPB built out its Paying for College website, with cost information on approximately 7,700 educational institutions.

PERFORMANCE GOAL

Engage the public by hosting public field hearings, town hall meetings, Consumer Advisory Board meetings, and other events on consumer finance issues.

TABLE 13: NUMBER OF PUBLIC HEARINGS, TOWN HALL MEETINGS, CONSUMER ADVISORY BOARD MEETINGS, AND OTHER PUBLIC EVENTS HOSTED ANNUALLY.

	FY 2013	FY 2014
Target	8 Events	9 Events
Actual	11 Events	13 Events

The Bureau hosted 13 public events in FY 2014, focused on key issues affecting consumer financial markets such as credit cards, mortgages, auto finance, and payday lending. These included three meetings of its Consumer Advisory Board. The Bureau also participated in dozens of public events hosted by others in FY 2014, including testifying before Congress on nine occasions to discuss policy, operations and budget matters.

1.3   Civil Penalty Fund Annual Report

Section 1055(a) of the Dodd-Frank Act authorizes the CFPB to obtain any appropriate legal or equitable relief for violations of Federal consumer financial laws. That relief may include civil penalties. Section 1017(d) of the Dodd-Frank Act further established a Consumer Financial Civil Penalty Fund (Civil Penalty Fund) into which the Bureau deposits civil penalties it collects in judicial and administrative actions under Federal consumer financial laws.

Under the Act, funds in the Civil Penalty Fund may be used for payments to the victims of activities for which civil penalties have been imposed under the Federal consumer financial laws. To the extent that such victims cannot be located or such payments are otherwise not practicable, the Bureau may use funds in the Civil Penalty Fund for the purpose of consumer education and financial literacy programs.

On May 7, 2013, the Bureau published the Civil Penalty Fund rule, 12 C.F.R. part 1075, a final rule governing the Bureau's use of the funds in the Civil Penalty Fund. That rule requires the Bureau to issue regular reports on the Civil Penalty Fund. Included in this Annual Report within the accompanying tables provided below are a list of all civil penalty collections from October 1, 2012 through September 30, 2014, the schedule for Civil Penalty Fund allocations, a description of Civil Penalty Fund allocations in FY 2013 and FY 2014 and the basis for those allocations, and an overview of the distribution of those funds.

Additional background information on the Civil Penalty Fund can be found at:
http://www.consumerfinance.gov/budget/civil-penalty-fund/

As of September 30, 2014 the Civil Penalty Fund has $112.8 million of funds available for future allocation to harmed consumers and/or financial education. Table 14 below summarizes significant activity of the fund since inception through September 30, 2014:

TABLE 14: CIVIL PENALTY FUND SIGNIFICANT ACTIVITY

Activity	Amount	Amount
Cash Collections:		
FY 2012		$32,000,000
FY 2013		$49,520,001
FY 2014		$77,502,001
Total Cash Collections		$159,022,002
Less Allocations:		
Victim Compensation		
FY 2013	$10,488,815	
FY 2014	$20,803,560	$31,292,375
Consumer Education and Financial Literacy Programs		
FY 2013	$13,380,000	
FY 2014	$0	$13,380,000
Total Allocations		$44,672,375
Less Administrative Set-aside:		
FY 2013		$1,573,322
Total Available for Future Allocations		**$112,776,305**

Civil Penalty Fund Collections

TABLE 15: FISCAL YEAR 2013 COLLECTIONS

Defendant name	Civil Penalty collected	Collection date
American Express Centurion Bank	$3,900,000	October 1, 2012
American Express, FSB	$1,200,000	October 1, 2012
American Express Travel	$9,000,000	October 1, 2012
Payday Loan Debt Solution, Inc.	$5,000	December 28, 2012
Abraham M. Pessar (Gordon, *et. al*)	$1	February 26, 2013
United Guaranty Corporation	$4,500,000	April 11, 2013
Genworth Mortgage Ins. Corp.	$4,500,000	April 15, 2013
Mortgage Guaranty Ins. Corp (MGIC)	$2,650,000	April 16, 2013
Radian Guaranty Inc.	$3,750,000	April 29, 2013
American Debt Settlement Solutions, Inc.	$15,000	June 12, 2013
JPMorgan Chase	$20,000,000	September 19, 2013
Total	**$49,520,001**	

In fiscal year 2013, the Bureau collected civil penalties from 11 defendants totaling $49.5 million.[1]

---

[1] In FY13 a civil money penalty for $1.1 million was imposed in the National Legal Help Center case. The civil penalty in this case is not reasonably expected to be received and has not resulted in accounts receivable.

TABLE 16: FISCAL YEAR 2014 COLLECTIONS

Defendant name	Civil Penalty Collected	Collection date
Washington Federal	$34,000	October 11, 2013
Mortgage Master, Inc.	$425,000	October 15, 2013
Castle & Cooke Mortgage, LLC	$4,000,000	November 13, 2013
Cash America International, Inc.	$5,000,000	November 25, 2013
Meracord, LLC.	$1,376,000[2]	November 26, 2013 July 16, 2014
Republic Mortgage Insurance Company	$100,000	December 5, 2013
American Express Bank, FSB	$2,000,000	December 23, 2013
American Express Centurion Bank	$3,600,000	December 23, 2013
American Express Travel Related Services	$4,000,000	December 23, 2013
Ally	$18,000,000	December 30, 2013
Fidelity Mortgage Corporation	$54,000	January 21, 2014
1st Alliance Lending, LLC	$83,000	March 5, 2014
Bank of America	$20,000,000	April 17, 2014
RealtySouth	$500,000	June 4, 2014
Synchrony (GE Capital Retail Bank)	$3,500,000	June 20, 2014
Stonebridge Title Services, Inc.	$30,000	June 24, 2014
Ace Cash Express, Inc.	$5,000,000	July 18, 2014
Colfax (Culver Capital, LLC)	$1	August 5, 2014

---

[2] Meracord LLC paid $1.4 million in civil penalties in two installments, $600,000 on November 26, 2013 and $800,000 on July 16, 2014.

USA Discounters, Ltd.	$50,000	August 19, 2014
Amerisave Mortgage Corporation	$6,000,000	August 22, 2014
First Investors Financial Services Group, Inc.	$2,750,000	August 29, 2014
Global Client Solutions	$1,000,000	September 5, 2014
Total	**$77,502,001**	

In fiscal year 2014, the Bureau collected civil penalties from 22 defendants totaling $77.5 million. [3]

Allocations from the Civil Penalty Fund

Under the Civil Penalty Fund rule, the Civil Penalty Fund Administrator allocates funds in the Civil Penalty Fund to classes of victims of violations of Federal consumer financial laws and, to the extent that such victims cannot be located or such payments are otherwise not practicable, to consumer education and financial literacy programs according to a schedule published by the Fund Administrator. That schedule established six-month periods and provides that an allocation will be made within 60 days of the end of each period. The Fund Administrator may allocate only those funds that were available as of the end of the six-month period and may allocate funds to a class of victims only if that class had uncompensated harm as of the end of the six-month period.

---

[3] Three additional civil penalty fund cases resulted in accounts receivable in Fiscal Year 2014, to be collected in early Fiscal Year 2015. These accounts receivable total $15.2 million. In particular, the Bureau expects civil penalty collections of $5 million from U.S. Bank, $200,000 from Lighthouse Title, and $10 million from Flagstar Bank, F.S.B. A civil penalty of $1 was imposed in the 3D-Resorts- Bluegrass, LLC case. The civil penalty in this case is not reasonably expected to be received and has not resulted in accounts receivable.

TABLE 17: SCHEDULE FOR ALLOCATIONS, PERIODS 1, 2, 3, AND 4

Period	Start	End	Allocation Deadline
1	July 21, 2011	March 31, 2013	May 30, 2013
2	April 1, 2013	September 30, 2013	November 29, 2013
3	October 1, 2013	March 31, 2014	May 30, 2014
4	April 1, 2014	September 30, 2014	November 29, 2014

The table displays the dates by which funds will be allocated following the first four six-month periods. Allocations must occur within 60 days after the end of each six-month period. Therefore, under the current schedule, subsequent allocations will also occur between April 1 and May 30 and between October 1 and November 29 of each year.

Allocations in FY 2013

Period 1: July 21, 2011 – March 31, 2013

The Bureau made its first allocation from the Civil Penalty Fund on May 30, 2013. As of March 31, 2013, $46.1 million was in the Civil Penalty Fund. Of that, $1.6 million was set aside for any administrative costs and $44.5 million was available for allocation under 12 C.F.R. § 1075.105(c).

TABLE 18: PERIOD 1: CASES IN WHICH A CIVIL PENALTY WAS IMPOSED

Defendant Name	Date of Final Order[4]
Capital One Bank	July 18, 2012
Discover	September 24, 2012
American Express Centurion Bank	October 1, 2012
American Express Bank, FSB	October 1, 2012
American Express Travel	October 1, 2012
Payday Loan Debt Solution, Inc.	December 21, 2012
Abraham M. Pessar (Gordon, *et. al*)	February 1, 2013

During Period 1, final orders in Bureau enforcement actions imposed civil penalties in seven cases. The table above lists the date of the final order in each of those cases. Under the Civil Penalty Fund rule, the victims of the violations for which the civil penalties were imposed in these cases are eligible to receive payment from the Civil Penalty Fund to compensate their uncompensated harm.

Of those cases, two cases—Payday Loan Debt Solution, Inc. (PLDS), and Gordon, *et al.*—had classes of victims with uncompensated harm that is compensable from the Civil Penalty Fund.[5]

---

[4] Under Section 1075.101 of the Civil Penalty Fund rule, for purposes of Civil Penalty Fund allocations, a "Final Order" is a consent order or settlement issued by a court or by the Bureau, or an appealable order issued by a court or by the Bureau as to which the time for filing an appeal has expired and no appeals are pending. Appeals include petitions for reconsideration, review, rehearing, and certiorari. For reporting purposes, "date of final order" for all consent orders is defined as the date the order was entered on the docket. The chart has been updated for all periods to reflect this definition. In our prior financial report, the "date of final order" in some instances reflected the date the final order was signed rather than the docket-entry date. No changes in allocation periods or fiscal year quarters have occurred as a result of this reporting update. For appealable orders, the "date of final order" is the date the order became final under federal law.

[5] Under the Civil Penalty Fund rule victims' compensable harm is determined by looking to the terms of the relevant court or administrative order. If the amount of a victim's compensable harm cannot be determined based on the terms of the relevant order, the victim's compensable harm generally will be his or her out-of-pocket losses that resulted from the violation. To determine the amount of a victim's uncompensated harm, the Bureau will take the

In particular, the PLDS victims had $488,815 in uncompensated harm, and the Gordon victims had $10 million in uncompensated harm. The victims in the other five cases had no uncompensated harm that was compensable from the Civil Penalty Fund.

The Bureau allocated $488,815 to the PLDS class of victims and $10 million to the Gordon class of victims, enough to compensate fully each class's uncompensated harm. After making that allocation, $34 million remained available for allocation. Of this figure, the Bureau allocated $13.4 million for consumer education and financial literacy programs.

Period 1 Allocation Summary:

Victim Compensation: $10,488,815

- Payday Loan Debt Solution, Inc.

  - Victim Class Allocation: $488,815

- Gordon, et al.

  - Victim Class Allocation: $10,000,000

Consumer Education and Financial Literacy Programs: $13,380,000

Total Allocation: $23,868,815

Allocations in FY 2014

Period 2: April 1, 2013 – September 30, 2013

On November 29, 2013, the Bureau made its second allocation from the Civil Penalty Fund. As of September 30, 2013, the Civil Penalty Fund contained an unallocated balance of $56.1 million. This amount was available for allocation pursuant to 12 C.F.R. § 1075.105(c).

---

victim's total compensable harm and subtract out any compensation that the victim has received—or is reasonably expected to receive—for that harm. See 12 C.F.R. § 1075.104.

TABLE 19: PERIOD 2: CASES IN WHICH A CIVIL PENALTY WAS IMPOSED

Defendant Name	Date of Final Order
United Guaranty Corporation	April 8, 2013
Genworth Mortgage Ins. Corp.	April 5, 2013
Mortgage Guaranty Ins. Corp. (MGIC)	April 5, 2013
Radian Guaranty Inc.	April 9, 2013
American Debt Settlement Solutions, Inc.	June 7, 2013
JPMorgan Chase	September 19, 2013
National Legal Help Center[6]	September 23, 2013

During Period 2, final orders in Bureau enforcement actions imposed civil penalties in seven cases. The table above lists the date that the order in each of those cases became a "final order" within the meaning of the Civil Penalty Fund rule. Under the Civil Penalty Fund rule, the victims of the violations for which the civil penalties were imposed in these cases are eligible to receive payment from the Civil Penalty Fund to compensate their uncompensated harm.

Of those seven cases, the Civil Penalty Fund Administrator determined that one case did not have a class of victims with uncompensated harm that is compensable from the Civil Penalty Fund, and that two cases included classes of victims with uncompensated harm that is compensable from the Civil Penalty Fund. As of the time of the allocation, the Fund Administrator did not yet have sufficient information to determine whether classes of victims in the remaining four cases had "compensable harm" or "uncompensated harm" as defined by the Civil Penalty Fund rule. The two cases with classes of victims with uncompensated harm that is compensable from the Civil Penalty Fund were American Debt Settlement Solutions, Inc. (ADSS) and National Legal Help Center (NLHC). Specifically, the ADSS victims had $499,248 in uncompensated harm and the NLHC victims had $2.1 million in uncompensated harm.

---

[6] In the National Legal Help Center case, the defendants were ordered to pay $1.1 million in civil monetary penalties. At the time of this report, the Bureau does not reasonably expect to receive these penalties.

The Bureau allocated $499,248 to two classes of victims in ADSS and $2.1 million to the NLHC class of victims, enough to compensate fully those victim classes' uncompensated harm. No funds were allocated to consumer education and financial literacy programs. The remaining unallocated Civil Penalty Fund balance remained available for future allocations.

Period 2 Allocation Summary:

Victim Compensation: $2,557,231

- American Debt Settlement Solutions, Inc.
  - Victim Classes Allocation: $499,248
- National Legal Help Center
  - Victim Class Allocation: $2,057,983

Consumer Education and Financial Literacy Programs: $0

Total Allocation: $2,557,231

Period 3: October 1, 2013- March 31, 2014

On May 30, 2014, the Bureau made its third allocation from the Civil Penalty Fund. As of March 31, 2014, the Civil Penalty Fund contained an unallocated balance of $91.4 million. This amount was available for allocation pursuant to 12 C.F.R. § 1075.105(c).

TABLE 20: PERIOD 3: CASES IN WHICH A CIVIL PENALTY WAS IMPOSED

Defendant Name	Date of Final Order
Meracord, LLC	October 4, 2013
Washington Federal	October 9, 2013
Mortgage Master, Inc.	October 9, 2013
Castle & Cooke Mortgage, LLC	November 12, 2013
Republic Mortgage Insurance Company	November 19, 2013
Cash America International, Inc.	November 21, 2013
3D Resorts- Bluegrass, LLC	December 3, 2013
Ally	December 20, 2013
American Express Bank, FSB	December 24, 2013
American Express Centurion Bank	December 24, 2013
American Express Travel Related Services	December 24, 2013
Fidelity Mortgage Corporation	January 16, 2014
1st Alliance Lending, LLC	February 24, 2014

During Period 3, final orders in Bureau enforcement actions imposed civil penalties in 13 cases. Under the Civil Penalty Fund rule, the victims of the violations for which the civil penalties were imposed in these cases are eligible to receive payment from the Civil Penalty Fund to compensate their uncompensated harm.

Of those cases, the Civil Penalty Fund Administrator determined that two cases did not have eligible classes of victims, and seven cases had classes of eligible victims with no uncompensated harm that is compensable from the Civil Penalty Fund. Additionally, as of the time of the Period 3 allocation, the Fund Administrator did not have sufficient information to determine whether classes of victims in one Period 3 case, along with four cases from Period 2, had "compensable harm" or "uncompensated harm" as defined in the Civil Penalty Fund rule.

Of the three cases that had classes of eligible victims with uncompensated harm, the classes of eligible victims with uncompensated harm in one case are expected to receive full compensation pursuant to an order issued by another federal regulator. The two remaining cases with classes of victims with uncompensated harm that is compensable from the Civil Penalty Fund were Meracord and 3D Resorts-Bluegrass. Specifically, the Meracord victims had $11.5 million in estimated uncompensated harm, and the 3D Resorts-Bluegrass victims had $6.7 million in estimated uncompensated harm.

The Bureau allocated $11.5 million to the Meracord victim class and $6.7 million to the 3D Resorts-Bluegrass victim class, enough to compensate fully those victim classes' uncompensated harm. No funds were allocated to consumer education and financial literacy programs. The remaining unallocated Civil Penalty Fund balance remains available for future allocation.

Period 3 Allocation Summary:

Victim Compensation: $18,246,329

- Meracord

  - Victim Class Allocation: $11,542,229

- 3D Resorts- Bluegrass

  - Victim Class Allocation: $6,704,100

Consumer Education and Financial Literacy Programs: $0

Total Allocation: $18,246,329

FY 2014 cases eligible for allocation in FY 2015

Period 4: March 31, 2014- September 30, 2014

On or before November 29, 2014, the Bureau will make its fourth allocation from the Civil Penalty Fund. As of September 30, 2014, the Civil Penalty Fund had an unallocated balance of $112.8 million. This amount will be available for allocation pursuant to 12 C.F.R. § 1075.105(c).

TABLE 21: PERIOD 4: CASES IN WHICH A CIVIL PENALTY WAS IMPOSED

Defendant Name	Date of Final Order
Bank of America	April 9, 2014
RealtySouth	May 28, 2014
Stonebridge Title Services, Inc.	June 12, 2014
Synchrony (GE Capital Retail Bank)	June 19, 2014
Ace Cash Express, Inc.	July 10, 2014
Colfax (Culver Capital, LLC)	July 29, 2014
Amerisave Mortgage Corporation	August 12, 2014
USA Discounters, Ltd.	August 14, 2014
First Investors Financial Services Group, Inc.	August 20, 2014
Global Client Solutions	August 27, 2014
U.S. Bank	September 25, 2014
Flagstar Bank, F.S.B.	September 29, 2014
Lighthouse Title	September 30, 2014

Civil Penalty Fund Distributions

Civil penalty fund distributions have begun for two Civil Penalty Fund allocations made in Period 1 and Period 2. These distribution figures reflect the amounts that have been mailed to harmed consumers; these distributions are still active and checks continue to be deposited by consumers. In the Payday Loan Debt Solution, Inc. case, $458,526 has been distributed to harmed consumers. In the American Debt Settlements Solutions, Inc. case $499,246 has been distributed to harmed consumers. Distributions are expected to begin in fiscal year 2015 for the Gordon, *et al.*, National Legal Help Center, Meracord, and 3D Resorts- Bluegrass LLC cases.

TABLE 22: CIVIL PENALTY FUND DISTRIBUTIONS

Defendant	Period	Distribution Amount
Payday Loan Debt Solution, Inc.	1	$458,526
American Debt Settlement Solutions, Inc.	2	$499,246

Bureau-Administered Redress

Dodd-Frank Act Section 1055 authorizes a court in a judicial action, or the CFPB in an administrative proceeding, to grant any appropriate legal or equitable relief for a violation of Federal consumer financial law. Such relief may include redress for victims of the violations, including refunds, restitution, and damages. Relief that is intended to compensate victims is treated as fiduciary funds and deposited into the "Legal or Equitable Relief Fund" established at the Department of the Treasury. CFPB refers to these collections as Bureau-Administered Redress.

Bureau-Administered Redress Collections

TABLE 23: COLLECTIONS IN FY 2013

Defendant	Amount Collected	Date of Collection
Payday Loan Debt Solution, Inc.	$100,000	December 28, 2012
Gordon, *et al*	$22,804	August 9, 2013

In Fiscal Year 2013, the Bureau collected $122,804 in Bureau-Administered Redress funds from two defendants. Funds for each case will be used to compensate victims in accordance with the terms of the final order for that case.[7]

TABLE 24: COLLECTIONS IN FY 2014

Defendant	Amount Collected	Date of Collection
Castle and Cooke	$9,228,896	November 13, 2013
3D Resorts- Bluegrass	$50,000	December 6, 2013
Amerisave	$14,892,234	August 15, 2014
Global Client Solutions	$4,000,000	September 5, 2014

In Fiscal Year 2014, the Bureau collected $28.2 million in Bureau-Administered Redress funds from four defendants.[8] In these cases, funds will be distributed in accordance with terms of the final order for each case.[9]

---

[7] For example, in the Payday Loan Debt Solution Inc. case the final order provides that the Bureau-Administered Redress funds should be used to pay restitution to victims and to cover attendant administrative expenses.

[8] Two Bureau-Administered Redress cases resulted in accounts receivable in Fiscal Year 2014, to be collected in Fiscal Year 2015 totaling $29.6 million. In particular, the Bureau expects to collect redress of $2.1 million from Global Client Solutions and $27.5 million from Flagstar Bank, F.S.B.

Bureau-Administered Redress Distributions

TABLE 25: BUREAU-ADMINISTERED REDRESS DISBURSEMENTS

Defendant	Quarter of Distribution	Amount Distributed
Payday Loan Debt Solution, Inc.	FY14 Q1	$76,442
Castle and Cooke Mortgage, LLC.	FY14 Q3	$9,175,596

In the first quarter of FY2014, Bureau-Administered Redress funds from the Payday Loan Debt Solution, Inc. case were distributed to eligible victims in accordance with the terms of the final order.[10] In the third quarter of FY 2014, Bureau-Administered Redress funds from the Castle and Cooke Mortgage, LLC case were distributed to eligible victims in accordance with the terms of the final order. In FY 2014, using Bureau-Administered Redress funds the Bureau distributed a total of $9.3 million to harmed consumers.

---

[9] In the Castle and Cooke, Amerisave, and Global Client Solution cases, the respective final orders provide that the Bureau-Administered Redress funds should be used to pay redress to victims and to cover attendant administrative expenses.

[10] The final order in the Payday Loan Debt Solution, Inc. case included two classes of victims. One class was compensated in accordance with the final order using Bureau-Administered Redress funds. The other class was compensated with an allocation and subsequent disbursement from the Civil Penalty Fund.

1.4 Management assurances and audit results

CFPB Statement of Management Assurance

Fiscal Year 2014, November 10, 2014

The management of the Consumer Financial Protection Bureau (CFPB) is responsible for establishing and maintaining effective internal control and financial management systems that meet the objectives of the Federal Managers' Financial Integrity Act of 1982 (FMFIA). Continuous monitoring and periodic evaluations provide the basis for the annual assessment and report on management's controls, as required by FMFIA. The FMFIA methodologies assist in assessing the applicable entity-wide controls, documenting the applicable processes, and identifying and testing the key controls. Based on the results of these ongoing evaluations, the CFPB is able to provide a qualified statement of assurance that the internal control over the effectiveness and efficiency of operations and compliance with applicable laws and regulations meet the objectives of FMFIA, with the exception of a material weakness identified as of September 30, 2014. We will continue to take appropriate steps to implement timely corrective actions.

As required by the Dodd-Frank Act, the CFPB is to provide a management assertion as to the effectiveness of the CFPB's internal control over financial reporting. The CFPB management is responsible for establishing and maintaining effective internal control over financial reporting. The CFPB conducted its assessment of the effectiveness of internal control over financial reporting based on the criteria established under 31 U.S.C. Sec. 3512(c) and applicable sections of OMB Circular A-123. Based on the results of this evaluation, a material weakness was identified in its internal control over financial reporting as of September 30, 2014. Other than the exception noted, the internal controls were operating effectively and no other material weaknesses were found in the design or operation of the internal control over financial reporting.

Under the Dodd-Frank Act, the CFPB is required to maintain financial management systems that comply substantially with Federal financial management systems requirements and applicable Federal accounting standards. The CFPB utilizes financial management systems that substantially comply with the requirements for Federal financial management systems and applicable Federal accounting standards.

Richard Cordray

Richard Cordray
Director of the Consumer Financial Protection Bureau

Federal Managers' Financial Integrity Act

The CFPB was established as an independent bureau in the Federal Reserve System under the Dodd-Frank Act Section 1011 (a). As an independent, non-appropriated bureau, CFPB recognizes the importance of Federal laws associated with implementing effective risk management, including the Federal Managers' Financial Integrity Act. This includes ensuring that CFPB operations and programs are effective and efficient and that internal controls are sufficient to minimize exposure to waste and mismanagement.

In fiscal year 2014, CFPB performed an evaluation of its risks and systems of internal controls. Based on the results of those evaluations, the CFPB is able to provide a qualified statement of assurance that the internal control over the effectiveness and efficiency of operations, and compliance with applicable laws and regulations meet the objectives of FMFIA, with the exception of one (1) material weakness and one (1) significant deficiency that were identified as of September 30, 2014, listed below. The CFPB is committed to continuously enhancing and improving its systems of internal control and realizing more effective and efficient ways to accomplish its mission; as well as taking appropriate steps to implement timely corrective actions.

Accounts Payable Accrual Process (*Material Weakness*)

A material weakness has been identified in the accounts payable accrual process. Although policies and procedures are in place around the accrual process, a number of errors continue to exist relating to the calculation of the accrual amounts for expenses and property and equipment and the OCFO review process over those accrual amounts. In fiscal year 2013, a significant deficiency was identified in the accounts payable accrual process. During fiscal year 2014, the OCFO implemented corrective actions to mitigate the risks of this deficiency: provided additional outreach and guidance to Contracting Officer Representatives (COR) and invoice approvers, implemented a sampling methodology to review the accrual amounts, and began developing a resource and desk guide for the CORs and invoice approvers. The corrective actions implemented did not mitigate the risks appropriately and the errors in the accounts payable accrual amounts resulted in the identification of a material weakness. During fiscal year 2015, the Bureau will implement steps to remediate these issues working with CORs, invoice approvers, and the Bureau's accountable officials. Such corrective actions will include the completion and dissemination of the resource and desk guide for the CORs and invoice approvers, more collaboration between the OCFO and the CORs and invoice approvers when calculating the accrual amounts, more oversight by the OCFO over the budget execution of contracts and interagency agreements which impact the associated accrual amounts, and a more comprehensive OCFO review process over the accrual amounts. Although it is our understanding that this material weakness does not indicate that the Bureau overspent its funds in FY 2014 (in fact it appears to have underspent them), the Bureau is committed to correcting the imprecision in the accrual estimation process to ensure the proper accounting and reporting of the Bureau's expenses.

Accounting for Property and Equipment (*Significant Deficiency***)**

A significant deficiency continues to be identified over the accounting for property and equipment. Although policies and procedures around the accounting for property and equipment are in place, a number of errors continue to exist relating to the proper capitalization or expensing of costs associated with the purchase of furniture and equipment or development of internal use software. In fiscal year 2013, a significant deficiency was identified in the accounting for property and equipment. During fiscal year 2014, the OCFO implemented corrective actions to mitigate the risks of this deficiency: provided additional outreach and guidance to CORs and invoice approvers and implemented a review process over contracts and interagency agreements for the purchase or development of items that may be capitalized. The corrective actions implemented did not fully mitigate the risks and therefore this significant deficiency is still identified in fiscal year 2014. During fiscal year 2015, the Bureau will increase its collaboration between the OCFO, applicable CORs and invoice approvers, and the Office of Procurement; continue its review over contracts and interagency agreements; and implement a process to more systematically gather and disseminate information on fixed asset acquisitions to ensure capitalized costs are accurately captured and recorded.

Additionally, the CFPB identified several enhancement areas to focus on and during fiscal year 2015 will continue to make progress toward: implementing a more comprehensive asset management process; implementing an enterprise risk management program; developing, reviewing, and revising policies and procedures as appropriate; fully implementing and enhancing the guidelines and processes around accruals and asset capitalization; developing a new performance management system and additional steps to promote fairness and inclusion in the workplace; carefully managing the headquarters renovation; providing leadership and management training, enhancing staff training and development programs and working towards the goal of being fully staffed; and enhancing the Bureau's Information Security Program.

Federal financial management systems requirements

Section 1017(a)(4)(C) of the Dodd-Frank Act requires the CFPB to implement and maintain financial management systems that substantially comply with Federal financial management systems requirements and applicable Federal accounting standards. The CFPB performs or is subject to a number of other assessments in order to further support compliance with the requirement set forth within the Dodd Frank Act requiring the CFPB to implement and maintain Financial Management Systems that comply substantially with the Federal Financial Management Systems requirements and applicable accounting standards. These assessments also assist in documenting compliance with the Federal Financial Management System requirements. Assessments include but are not limited to:

- Internal Control over Financial Reporting (ICOFR)
- Federal Information Security Management Act (FISMA)
- Improper Payments
- Annual Financial Statement Audit
- Federal Manager's Financial Integrity Act Reporting of 1982 (FMFIA)
- Federal Financial Management Improvement Act of 1996 (FFMIA)

Based on the results of these internal control assessments, the CFPB provided reasonable assurance that as of September 30, 2014:

- The CFPB financial management systems substantially comply with the requirements for Federal financial management systems and applicable Federal accounting standards.

Additionally, as discussed in the section on Financial Management System Strategy below, the CFPB has entered into an agreement with the Bureau of Fiscal Services, Administrative Resource Center (BFS/ARC) for the cross-servicing of the CFPB's core financial management system needs. As such, BFS/ARC has provided assurances to the CFPB that BFS/ARC's system is in compliance with the Federal Financial Management Improvement Act (FFMIA) whereby the system is substantially compliant with:

- Federal financial management system requirements,

- Applicable federal accounting standards, and

- The United States Standard General Ledger at the transaction level.

BFS/ARC has reported that its system substantially complies with these three requirements of FFMIA and recently completed a Statement on Standards for Attestation Engagement (SSAE) No. 16, Reporting on Controls at a Service Organization. The independent auditors opined in the SSAE-16 report that BFS/ARC's controls were suitably designed to provide reasonable assurance that control objectives would be achieved if customer agencies applied the complementary customer agency controls.

The CFPB evaluated its internal controls over the processing of transactions between the CFPB and BFS/ARC. The CFPB has determined it has adequate complementary customer controls in place.

Financial statement audit and report on internal control over financial reporting

Sections 1017(a)(4)(B) and (D) of the Dodd-Frank Act require the CFPB to prepare and submit to GAO annual financial statements and an assertion of the effectiveness of the internal control over financial reporting. Section 1017(a)(5)(A) and (B) of the Dodd-Frank Act also require GAO to audit those financial statements and report their results to the Bureau, Congress and the President. The CFPB prepared comparative financial statements for fiscal years 2013 and 2014.

GAO issued an unmodified or "clean" audit opinion on the CFPB's fiscal years 2013 and 2014 financial statements. GAO opined that due to a material weakness in internal control over the reporting of accounts payable, the CFPB did not maintain, in all material respects, effective internal control over financial reporting as of September 30, 2014. However, GAO reported that its tests for compliance with selected provisions of applicable laws, regulations, contracts, and grant agreements disclosed no instances of noncompliance for fiscal year 2014 that would be reported under U.S. generally accepted government auditing standards.

Financial management systems strategy

The CFPB recognized during its initial years of operation that it needed to leverage from other federal agencies existing financial management resources, systems and information technology platforms. Initially, all of the CFPB's financial management transactions were processed through the Department of the Treasury's Departmental Offices. The Bureau also relied on Treasury for much of its information technology infrastructure. The CFPB has maintained an agreement with the BFS for the cross-servicing of a commercial off-the-shelf core financial management system designed and configured to meet generally accepted accounting principles for Federal entities. In addition to the core financial management system, BFS provides services that include transactional processing, financial reporting, human resource services, procurement services, and travel services. The CFPB's goal is to continue providing an effective strategy that supports our financial management systems.

The CFPB recognizes the importance of financial management systems and oversight as a part of the capital planning and investment control process. Accordingly, the CFPB relies on its Investment Review Board (IRB) as the executive advisory body responsible for ensuring that all business and technology investments are aligned to the CFPB's mission, vision, strategic goals and initiatives, and utilize program management best practices to achieve the maximum return on investments. The IRB is chaired by the Chief Financial Officer (CFO). Investments over $0.5 million are reviewed by the IRB, unless waived by the Chair in consultation with IRB members. The Chair may require IRB review of investments less than $0.5 million if the investment is deemed significant.

Federal Information Security Management Act

The Federal Information Security Management Act (FISMA) requires Federal agencies to develop, document, and implement an agency-wide program to provide security for the information and information systems that support the operations and assets of the agency. The CFPB has developed a Cyber Security Program in accordance with FISMA that is grounded in a foundation of well-documented policies, standards and processes. The Bureau relies on the soundness of this program to conduct reviews of its third-party service organizations including other federal entities with whom we have cross servicing agreements that enable us to leverage their existing information technology and platforms. As the CFPB continues to mature and grow, the security program will adjust as well to ensure the safety and protection of the Bureau's data and assets.

Improper payments

The Improper Payments Elimination and Recovery Act of 2011 (IPERA) requires agencies to review their programs and activities annually to identify those susceptible to significant improper payments. While the CFPB's Bureau Fund is not subject to the Act, in the interest of being consistent with government best practices, the Office of the Chief Financial Officer conducted such a review of five areas of payments during fiscal year 2014 – Purchase Card, Contract Payments and/or Invoices, Travel Card, Claims and/or Vouchers and Payroll. The

CFPB's risk assessment process did not identify any programs susceptible to significant improper payments.

The Civil Penalty Fund is subject to the Act. In fiscal year 2013, the CFPB made no disbursements from the Civil Penalty Fund. In fiscal year 2014, disbursements did not meet the reporting threshold for the Act.

Limitations of the Financial Statements

The principal financial statements contained in this report have been prepared to present the financial position and results of operations of the CFPB pursuant to the requirements of the Dodd-Frank Act Section 1017(a)(4)(B). While the statements have been prepared from the books and records of the Consumer Financial Protection Bureau, in accordance with generally accepted accounting principles for the Federal government, and follow the general presentation guidance provided by OMB, the statements are in addition to the financial reports used to monitor and control budgetary resources, which are prepared using the same books and records. The statements should be read with the understanding that they are for a component of the U.S. Government, a sovereign entity.

1.5 Financial analysis

Analysis of FY 2014 Financial Condition and Results

Since its inception in 2011 the Bureau has experienced considerable growth in the number of its employees, in the maturity of its processes and activities, and in the consumption of requested resources to conduct its activities. This is reflected in the data provided in Table 26 below that reports on significant changes between fiscal years 2014 and 2013.

TABLE 26: SUMMARY OF FINANCIAL INFORMATION

(In Dollars)	Percentage Change	FY 2014	FY 2013
Total Assets	41%	$687,481,254	$485,889,146
Total Liabilities	90%	$149,420,380	$78,579,861
Total Net Position	32%	$538,060,874	$407,309,285
Total Net Cost of Operations	27%	$497,553,748	$391,324,842
Total Budgetary Resources	12%	$796,718,485	$708,690,708
Total Obligations Incurred	-7%	$499,812,046	$538,759,116
Total Outlays	21%	$432,475,653	$356,591,467

Total Assets are $687.5 million as of September 30, 2014, an increase of $201.6 million (or 41 percent) over fiscal year 2013. The main factors contributing to the net increase are collections into the Bureau Fund ($91 million increase in Investments of the Bureau Fund) and the Civil Penalty Fund ($75.5 million increase in the Civil Penalty Fund balance). The Bureau's accounts receivable increased significantly in fiscal year 2014 (from $54,883 to $15.4 million) due to Civil Penalties imposed by the Bureau in fiscal year 2014 but not yet collected as of September 30, 2014. (The collections occurred in October 2014, after the closing date of the 2014 statements, see Note 18). Property and equipment increased from $27.7 million to $37.5 million (an increase of 35 percent), resulting primarily from the addition of assets related to software development and the leasehold improvement project.

Total Liabilities are $149.4 million as of September 30, 2014, an increase of $70.8 million (or 90 percent) over fiscal year 2013. The Bureau's liabilities generally represent the resources due to others such as benefits owed to employees and payments owed to vendors and Federal agencies for goods and services provided. Liabilities also include victim compensation amounts allocated from the Civil Penalty Fund (net of distributions to date), which increased from $13 million in 2013 to $30.3 million in fiscal year 2014.

Total Net Position at the end of fiscal year 2014 increased by $130.8 million from fiscal year 2013 as a result of the Bureau's total financing sources exceeding the cost of operations. While both the financing sources and cost of operations increased in 2014 due to the general growth of the agency, the increase in the net position is primarily due to activity in the Civil Penalty Fund, where Civil Monetary Penalties increased from about $49.5 million imposed in fiscal year 2013 to over $92.7 million imposed in fiscal year 2014, an increase in non-exchange revenue of $43.2 million. A similar increase is reflected in **Total Budgetary Resources**.

Total Net Cost of Operations increased in fiscal year 2014 from $391.3 million to $497.6 million (an increase of $106.2 million or 27 percent) due to the growth of the agency in each of its four strategic goals: (1) Prevent Financial Harm to Consumers While Promoting Good Practices That Benefit Them; (2) Empower Consumers to Live Better Financial Lives; (3) Inform the Public, Policy Makers, and the CFPB's own Policy-Making with Data-Driven Analysis of Consumer Finance Markets and Consumer Behavior; and, (4) Advance the CFPB's Performance by Maximizing Resources Productivity and Enhancing Impact. The largest increase in program cost in fiscal year 2014 supported the strategic goal of preventing financial harm to consumers while promoting good practices that benefit them. This goal includes the Bureau's rulemaking and enforcement activities for the consumer financial market.

How the CFPB is funded and other sources of revenue and collections

Bureau fund

Under the Dodd-Frank Act, the CFPB is funded principally by transfers from the Board of Governors of the Federal Reserve System up to a limit set forth in the statute. The CFPB requests transfers from the Board of Governors in amounts that are reasonably necessary to carry out its mission. Funding is capped at a pre-set percentage of the total 2009 operating expenses of the Federal Reserve System, subject to an annual adjustment. Specifically, the CFPB fund transfers are capped as follows:

- In fiscal year 2011, up to 10 percent of these Federal Reserve System expenses (or approximately $498 million),

- In fiscal year 2012, up to 11 percent of these expenses (or approximately $547.8 million),

- In fiscal year 2013, up to 12 percent of these expenses (or approximately $597.6 million), and

- In fiscal year 2014 and beyond, the cap remains at 12 percent but will be adjusted annually based on the percentage increase in the employment cost index for total compensation for State and local government workers published by the Federal Government.

The Dodd-Frank Act requires the CFPB to maintain an account with the Federal Reserve – "Bureau of Consumer Financial Protection Fund" (Bureau Fund). Funds requested from the Board of Governors are transferred into the Bureau Fund. Bureau funds determined not to be needed to meet the current needs of the CFPB are invested in Treasury securities on the open market. Earnings from the investments are also deposited into this fund. During fiscal year 2014 four transfers totaling $534 million were received from the Board of Governors. The amount transferred from the Board of Governors to the CFPB was $74 million less than the funding cap of $608 million, and $36 million less than the $570 million budget for fiscal year 2014.

The Dodd-Frank Act explicitly provides that Bureau funds obtained by or transferred to the CFPB are not Government funds or appropriated funds.

Civil Penalty Fund

As discussed previously in Section 1.3 of this report entitled, "Civil Penalty Fund Annual Report," the CFPB collected civil penalties from judicial or administrative actions in the amount of $77.5 million for fiscal year 2014 and $49.5 million for fiscal year 2013.

Other collections

During fiscal year 2014, the CFPB collected $149,600 in filing fees pursuant to the Interstate Land Sales Full Disclosure Act of 1968. The fees were deposited into an account maintained by the Department of the Treasury, and are retained and available until expended for the purpose of covering all or part of the costs that the Bureau incurs to operate the Interstate Land Sales program.

Fiduciary activity and custodial revenue

Dodd-Frank Act section 1055 authorizes a court in a judicial action, or the CFPB in an administrative proceeding, to grant any appropriate legal or equitable relief for a violation of Federal consumer financial law. Such relief may include redress for victims of the violations, including refunds, restitution, and damages. Relief that is intended to compensate victims is treated as fiduciary funds and deposited into the "Legal or Equitable Relief Fund" established at the Department of the Treasury. Fiduciary assets are not assets of the CFPB and are not recognized on the balance sheet. During fiscal year 2014, the CFPB collected $28.2 million in redress to be administered by the CFPB. Further information is contained in our financial statements at Note 19 entitled, "Fiduciary Activities."

Further, section 1055 of the Act provides that the CFPB may obtain the remedy of disgorgement for a violation of Federal consumer law. Disgorgement paid by the defendant is treated by CFPB as custodial revenue and maintained in the Miscellaneous Receipts Fund of the U.S. Treasury. CFPB reported the fiscal year 2014 disgorged deposits of $27,076 and any other miscellaneous funds collected or receivable (e.g., FOIA fees of $18,841) on the Statement of Custodial Activity – a statement that displays all custodial revenue for fiscal year 2013.

TABLE 27: OVERALL SUMMARY OF CFPB REVENUE AND RECEIPTS BY TYPE AND FISCAL YEAR

Fiscal Year	Transfers requested	Civil Penalty Fund receipts	Fiduciary receipts	Custodial revenue
2014	$533,800,000	$77,502,001	$28,231,130	$45,694
2013	$518,400,000	$49,520,001	$122,804	$128,201

What the CFPB has funded

As the CFPB migrated from its start-up efforts towards a steady state status as an entity during fiscal year 2014; many of its obligations related to resources essential to operations and activities such as personnel, information technology, mission-specific and human capital support, and other general support service activities. The CFPB incurred $499.8 million in obligations[11] – $259 million in Contracts & Support Services [12], $237 million in Salary & Benefits, and $4 million in All Other.

FIGURE 4:   FISCALYEAR 2014 OBLIGATIONS INCURRED ($ IN MILLIONS)

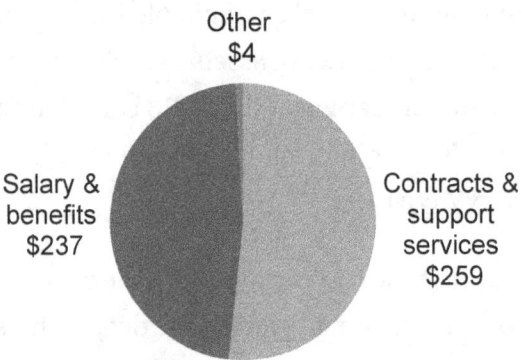

Examples of some of the larger obligations incurred for CFPB's fiscal year 2014 activities included in the $259 million for contracts and support services include:

- Assets in development, such as:

  o $6.9 million for supervisory compliance tools that will automate data analysis by providing functionality for examiners to analyze specific loan files in the field.

  o $22.9 million for maintaining ongoing operations of CFPB's consumer contact center and enhancements to the case management database;

- $22.8 million to the Department of the Treasury, Departmental Offices for various services such as information technology and human resource systems support;

---

[11] Obligations incurred amount of $499.8 million that is reported here and on the Statement of Budgetary Resources, includes $4.8 million in upward adjustments to prior year obligations, and $495 million associated with the fiscal year 2014 budget.

[12] Includes $104.7 million of interagency agreements (IAA) CFPB entered into with other Federal agencies. IAA's are not reported in USASpending.gov

- $7.5 million in agreements with the Board of Governors of the Federal Reserve System to provide Office of Inspector General services; and

- $12.1 million to the BFS/ARC and the Department of the Treasury Franchise Fund for cross-servicing of various human resource and financial management services, such as core financial accounting, transaction processing and reporting, travel, payroll and various IT services.

Net costs of the CFPB's operations

The Statement of Net Cost presents the CFPB net cost for its four strategic goals: (1) Prevent Financial Harm to Consumers While Promoting Good Practices That Benefit Them; (2) Empower Consumers to Live Better Financial Lives; (3) Inform the Public, Policy Makers, and the CFPB's own Policy-Making with Data-Driven Analysis of Consumer Finance Markets and Consumer Behavior; and, (4) Advance the CFPB's Performance by Maximizing Resources Productivity and Enhancing Impact. Net program costs for fiscal year 2014 are displayed in the chart below.

FIGURE 5: FISCAL YEAR 2014 NET PROGRAM COSTS ($ IN MILLIONS) `

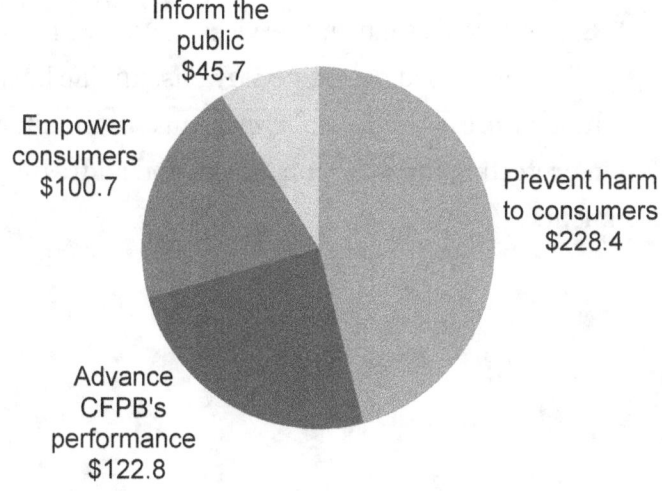

1.6   Possible future risks and uncertainties

Funding and independence

The Congress, in implementing the Dodd-Frank Act, followed a long-established precedent in providing the CFPB with sources of funding outside of the Congressional appropriations process to ensure full independence as the Bureau supervises and regulates providers of consumer financial products and services and protects financial consumers. Congress has consistently provided for independent sources of funding for Federal banking supervisors to allow for long-term planning and the execution of complex initiatives and to ensure that financial institutions are examined regularly and thoroughly for compliance with the law.

The CFPB has been tasked with supervising more entities than all other Federal bank supervisors combined, including supervising the largest, most complex banks. Effective supervision that assures a level playing field between bank and non-bank institutions requires dedicated and predictable resources and independent examiners. However, the CFPB is nonetheless the only banking supervisor with a statutory cap on its primary source of funding.

Possible future impact on financial services environment

It is anticipated that markets in both U.S. and foreign financial services sectors will evolve to address different and ever-changing implications based on their programs, unique business mixes, and organizational structures. These future external challenges must be monitored, as they will impact the work of the CFPB in protecting financial consumers and addressing a continually changing financial environment.

2. Financial Statements and Note Disclosures

Message from the Chief Financial Officer

During fiscal year 2014, the Office of the Chief Financial Officer (OCFO) continued to provide support for the Consumer Financial Protection Bureau (CFPB). Fiscal year 2014 marked a significant transition from the Bureau's initial years' status, most appropriately characterized as one of continued growth and maturity towards its goal of achieving a steady state status as a Federal agency. While the rate of growth has slowed during fiscal year 2014, CFPB still required significant attention to the growth and  maturity of its workforce, resources, and support contracts that facilitate the work of the only Federal agency with the sole focus of protecting the rights of financial consumers and enforcing Federal financial consumer laws.

The OCFO made numerous improvements to CFPB's financial management processes and enhanced the reporting of financial management results to CFPB decision makers and interested stakeholders. Three major actions included:

- Coordinating with the Bureau of Fiscal Services on the migration and training for travelers and supervisors to a new travel system and new processes for the decentralized review and approval of travel by immediate supervisors;
- Coordinating the receipt, management and disbursement of monies in the Civil Penalty Fund and the Legal or Equitable Relief Fund resulting from the actions of various defendants who violated Federal financial consumer laws; and,
- Continuing to provide program managers with monthly and quarterly financial data and information such as the status of funds for relevant programs, key investments, staffing status, and the availability to request funds for unanticipated needs.

Provided are the CFPB's financial statements as an integral part of the fiscal year 2014 Financial Report. For fiscal year 2014, the Government Accountability Office (GAO) rendered an unmodified or "clean" audit opinion on the CFPB's financial statements and noted one (1) material weakness regarding the accounts payable accruals process and one (1) significant deficiency regarding the recordation of property and equipment in the CFPB's internal control and cited no instances of non-compliance with laws and regulations. The OCFO will implement changes to the accounts payable accruals process and the property and equipment recordation process in fiscal year 2015 to remediate the issues identified by the GAO. The OCFO will work closely with the Chief Procurement Officer and the Contracting Officer Representatives, as well as other Bureau accountable officials to successfully remediate this material weakness and significant deficiency.

Stephen J. Agostini

2.1 U.S. Government Accountability Office auditor's report

441 G St. N.W.
Washington, DC 20548

Independent Auditor's Report

To the Director of the Bureau of Consumer Financial Protection

In our audits of the fiscal years 2014 and 2013 financial statements of the Bureau of Consumer Financial Protection, known as the Consumer Financial Protection Bureau (CFPB), we found

- the CFPB financial statements as of and for the fiscal years ended September 30, 2014, and 2013, are presented fairly, in all material respects, in accordance with U.S. generally accepted accounting principles;
- CFPB's internal control over financial reporting was not effective as of September 30, 2014; and
- no reportable noncompliance for fiscal year 2014 with provisions of applicable laws, regulations, contracts, and grant agreements we tested.

The following sections discuss in more detail (1) our report on the financial statements and on internal control over financial reporting, which includes required supplementary information (RSI)[1] and other information[2] included with the financial statements; (2) our report on compliance with laws, regulations, contracts, and grant agreements; and (3) agency comments.

Report on the Financial Statements and on Internal Control over Financial Reporting

As required by the Dodd-Frank Wall Street Reform and Consumer Protection Act[3] and the Full-Year Continuing Appropriations Act, 2011,[4] we have audited CFPB's financial statements. CFPB's financial statements comprise the balance sheets as of September 30, 2014, and 2013; the related statements of net cost of operations, changes in net position, budgetary resources, and custodial activity for the fiscal years then ended; and the related notes to the financial statements. We also have audited CFPB's internal control over financial reporting as of September 30, 2014, based on criteria established under 31 U.S.C. § 3512(c), commonly known as the Federal Managers' Financial Integrity Act (FMFIA), and applicable sections of Office of Management and Budget (OMB) Circular A-123, *Management's Responsibility for Internal Control.*

We conducted our audits in accordance with U.S. generally accepted government auditing standards. We believe that the audit evidence we obtained is sufficient and appropriate to provide a basis for our audit opinions.

---

[1]RSI consists of Management's Discussion and Analysis, which is included with the financial statements.

[2]Other information consists of information included with the financial statements, other than the RSI and the auditor's report.

[3]Pub. L. No. 111-203, § 1017(a)(5), 124 Stat. 1376, 1976-1977 (2010), codified at 12 U.S.C. § 5497(a)(5).

[4]Pub. L. No. 112-10, § 1573(a), 125 Stat 38, 138 (2011), codified at 12 U.S.C. § 5496a.

Management's Responsibility

CFPB management is responsible for (1) the preparation and fair presentation of these financial statements in accordance with U.S. generally accepted accounting principles; (2) preparing, measuring, and presenting the RSI in accordance with U.S. generally accepted accounting principles; (3) preparing and presenting other information included in documents containing the audited financial statements and auditor's report, and ensuring the consistency of that information with the audited financial statements and the RSI; (4) maintaining effective internal control over financial reporting, including the design, implementation, and maintenance of internal control relevant to the preparation and fair presentation of financial statements that are free from material misstatement, whether due to fraud or error; (5) evaluating the effectiveness of internal control over financial reporting based on the criteria established under FMFIA and applicable sections of OMB Circular A-123; and (6) providing its assertion about the effectiveness of internal control over financial reporting as of September 30, 2014, based on its evaluation, included in the accompanying Management's Report on Internal Control over Financial Reporting in appendix I.

Auditor's Responsibility

Our responsibility is to express an opinion on these financial statements and an opinion on CFPB's internal control over financial reporting based on our audits. U.S. generally accepted government auditing standards require that we plan and perform the audits to obtain reasonable assurance about whether the financial statements are free from material misstatement, and whether effective internal control over financial reporting was maintained in all material respects. We are also responsible for applying certain limited procedures to the RSI and other information included with the financial statements.

An audit of financial statements involves performing procedures to obtain audit evidence about the amounts and disclosures in the financial statements. The procedures selected depend on the auditor's judgment, including the auditor's assessment of the risks of material misstatement of the financial statements, whether due to fraud or error. In making those risk assessments, the auditor considers internal control relevant to the entity's preparation and fair presentation of the financial statements in order to design audit procedures that are appropriate in the circumstances. An audit of financial statements also involves evaluating the appropriateness of the accounting policies used and the reasonableness of significant accounting estimates made by management, as well as evaluating the overall presentation of the financial statements. An audit of internal control over financial reporting includes obtaining an understanding of internal control over financial reporting, assessing the risk that a material weakness exists,[5] evaluating the design and operating effectiveness of internal control over financial reporting based on the assessed risk, and testing relevant internal control over financial reporting. Our audit of internal control also considered the entity's process for evaluating and reporting on internal control over financial reporting based on criteria established under FMFIA and applicable sections of OMB Circular A-123. Our audits also included performing such other procedures as we considered necessary in the circumstances.

---

[5] A material weakness is a deficiency, or combination of deficiencies, in internal control over financial reporting, such that there is a reasonable possibility that a material misstatement of the entity's financial statements will not be prevented, or detected and corrected, on a timely basis. A deficiency in internal control exists when the design or operation of a control does not allow management or employees, in the normal course of performing their assigned functions, to prevent, or detect and correct, misstatements on a timely basis.

We did not evaluate all internal controls relevant to operating objectives as broadly established under FMFIA, such as those controls relevant to preparing performance information and ensuring efficient operations. We limited our internal control testing to testing controls over financial reporting. Our internal control testing was for the purpose of expressing an opinion on whether effective internal control over financial reporting was maintained, in all material respects. Consequently, our audit may not identify all deficiencies in internal control over financial reporting that are less severe than a material weakness.

Definitions and Inherent Limitations of Internal Control over Financial Reporting

An entity's internal control over financial reporting is a process effected by those charged with governance, management, and other personnel, the objectives of which are to provide reasonable assurance that (1) transactions are properly recorded, processed, and summarized to permit the preparation of financial statements in accordance with U.S. generally accepted accounting principles, and assets are safeguarded against loss from unauthorized acquisition, use, or disposition, and (2) transactions are executed in accordance with laws governing the use of budget authority and with other applicable laws, regulations, contracts, and grant agreements that could have a direct and material effect on the financial statements.

Because of its inherent limitations, internal control over financial reporting may not prevent, or detect and correct, misstatements due to fraud or error. We also caution that projecting any evaluation of effectiveness to future periods is subject to the risk that controls may become inadequate because of changes in conditions, or that the degree of compliance with the policies or procedures may deteriorate.

Opinion on Financial Statements

In our opinion, CFPB's financial statements present fairly, in all material respects, CFPB's financial position as of September 30, 2014, and 2013, and its net cost of operations, changes in net position, budgetary resources, and custodial activity for the fiscal years then ended in accordance with U.S. generally accepted accounting principles.

However, misstatements may nevertheless occur in other financial information reported by CFPB and not be detected as a result of the internal control deficiencies described in this report.

Opinion on Internal Control over Financial Reporting

In our opinion, because of a material weakness in internal control over the reporting of accounts payable, CFPB did not maintain, in all material respects, effective internal control over financial reporting as of September 30, 2014, based on criteria established under FMFIA and applicable sections of OMB Circular A-123.

Despite the material weakness in CFPB's internal control over reporting of accounts payable, CFPB made necessary and appropriate adjustments to its records and was therefore able to prepare financial statements that were fairly presented in all material respects for fiscal year 2014. However, the material weakness may adversely affect any decisions by CFPB's management that are based, in whole or in part, on information that is inaccurate because of this weakness. The issues constituting this material weakness, which are discussed in more detail below, were also disclosed by CFPB in its fiscal year 2014 (1) FMFIA assurance statement and (2) Management's Report on Internal Control over Financial Reporting. We considered this material weakness in determining the nature, timing, and extent of our audit procedures on CFPB's fiscal year 2014 financial statements.

In addition, we found that although CFPB took actions to attempt to address a significant deficiency in internal control over accounting for property and equipment that we reported in fiscal year 2013, our fiscal year 2014 audit continued to identify deficiencies in this area. These deficiencies, while not considered a material weakness, are important enough to merit the attention of those charged with governance of CFPB. Therefore, we considered these deficiencies over accounting for property and equipment collectively to be a significant deficiency in CFPB's internal control over financial reporting in fiscal year 2014.[6] This significant deficiency is discussed in more detail later in this report.

In addition to the material weakness and significant deficiency in internal control, we also identified other deficiencies in CFPB's internal control over financial reporting that we do not consider to be material weaknesses or significant deficiencies. Nonetheless, these deficiencies warrant CFPB management's attention. We have communicated these matters to CFPB management and, where appropriate, will report on them separately.

Material Weakness in Internal Control over Reporting of Accounts Payable

During our fiscal year 2014 audit, we found serious control deficiencies that affected CFPB's determination and reporting of accounts payable accruals. Specifically, we found that CFPB did not have effective procedures in place to determine and record an appropriate amount for goods and services received but not yet paid for as of September 30, 2014. Additionally, CFPB did not have effective review procedures to timely detect and correct inaccuracies in the accrual amounts.

CFPB's accounts payable balance consists primarily of amounts owed for goods and services received relating to contracts and property and equipment acquisitions that have not been paid. CFPB's accounts payable balance (including both intragovernmental and amounts due to the public) increased 75 percent from $32 million in fiscal year 2013 to approximately $56 million in fiscal year 2014. CFPB's Office of the Chief Financial Officer (OCFO) is responsible for the accrual process. CFPB's established procedures state that the OCFO sends a report to the contracting officer representative (COR) (for contracts) and invoice approver (for interagency agreements) of each division or program office, asking each to respond with an amount for services provided or goods received through the end of each quarter, for which CFPB has not received an invoice. The COR and invoice approver are then responsible for estimating an amount for each contract or interagency agreement, respectively, that should be accrued as of the end of each quarter. On a quarterly basis, the OCFO reviews financial documents, such as open obligation and accrual reports, to ensure completeness and accuracy of accruals submitted by the CORs and invoice approvers.

In our fiscal year 2013 audit opinion, we reported on a significant deficiency with respect to reporting accounts payable.[7] Consequently, we separately reported the details of the significant deficiency, along with recommendations for corrective actions, in May 2014.[8] Based on these recommendations, with which it concurred, CFPB took actions in an attempt to improve the

---

[6]A significant deficiency is a deficiency, or a combination of deficiencies, in internal control that is less severe than a material weakness, yet important enough to merit attention by those charged with governance.

[7]GAO, Financial Audit: Bureau of Consumer Financial Protection's Fiscal Years 2013 and 2012 Financial Statements, GAO-14-170R (Washington, D.C.: Dec. 16, 2013).

[8]GAO, Management Report: Improvements Needed in CFPB's Internal Controls and Accounting Procedures, GAO-14-455R (Washington, D.C.: May 2, 2014).

reporting of accounts payable. Such actions included (1) holding meetings with the CORs and invoice approvers to discuss responsibilities and challenges with the accounts payable accrual process, (2) requesting additional information and documentation from the CORs and invoice approvers to support the accrual amounts, (3) sampling accruals using a risk-based approach to perform reasonableness reviews, and (4) developing a guide for the CORs and invoice approvers discussing topics such as roles, responsibilities, accruals, open obligations, and fixed assets.

However, as of the end of our fiscal year 2014 audit, the guidance for the CORs and invoice approvers was still in draft form. Our fiscal year 2014 testing results showed that the CORs and invoice approvers continued to make errors in determining the amount of accounts payable to be accrued for reporting purposes. Specifically, we found multiple instances in which the CORs did not adequately estimate the amount owed for goods and services received as of September 30, 2014, and the OCFO reviews were not effective in detecting and correcting the errors. Based on our testing of a statistical sample of 42 accounts payable accruals, we found that CFPB incorrectly recorded approximately $3.2 million for nine sample items that represented goods and services that had already been received and paid for as of September 30, 2014. We also identified five accruals totaling $0.9 million for goods and services that had not yet been received in fiscal year 2014. In total, we identified 14 errors in our statistical sample of 42 that resulted in an overstatement to accounts payable of approximately $4.1 million. Most of these errors occurred as a result of the accounts payable accruals not being adjusted once the invoices were approved and paid. Because the OCFO's sampling methodology to review accruals was implemented in the third quarter of fiscal year 2014 and included only the 10 largest accrual amounts, it was not effective at detecting these errors.

After we brought these errors to CFPB's attention, CFPB management conducted an analysis to identify additional instances in which accounts payable accruals could have been misstated. We reviewed CFPB's analysis in relation to our testing results and determined that it was reasonable. Based on its analysis, CFPB reduced its accounts payable balance by $7.7 million. However, the cumulative impact of these continuing control deficiencies is such that a reasonable possibility exists that a material misstatement of CFPB's financial statements would not be prevented, or detected and corrected, on a timely basis. Consequently, these control deficiencies collectively represent a material weakness in CFPB's internal control over reporting of accounts payable.

These serious deficiencies in internal control over reporting of accounts payable are likely to continue to exist until CFPB (1) finalizes, disseminates, and implements detailed guidance to the CORs and invoice approvers; (2) provides continuous and effective training for the CORs and invoice approvers; and (3) strengthens its methodology to review accounts payable accruals. Because CFPB continues to grow as an agency, which has resulted in higher volumes of transactions each year, it is imperative that it address these issues in an effective and timely manner.

Significant Deficiency in Internal Control over Accounting for Property and Equipment

During our fiscal year 2014 audit, we continued to find that CFPB did not effectively implement internal controls over the recording of its property and equipment, which led to significant, but not material, misstatements in its financial statements. Specifically, we found that CFPB did not have effective procedures to properly distinguish between costs that should be recorded as property and equipment and those that should be recorded as gross costs (i.e., expensed) and appropriately record them in its financial records. Additionally, CFPB did not have effective review procedures to timely detect and correct errors in its records.

CFPB's property and equipment consist of internal-use software, internal-use software in development, general-purpose furniture and equipment, and leasehold improvements in development. During fiscal year 2014, CFPB acquired approximately $15 million in property and equipment. CFPB policy requires capitalizing property and equipment with estimated useful lives of 2 or more years that meet the following criteria: internal-use software purchased or developed of $750,000 or more; leasehold improvements and equipment acquisitions of $50,000 or more; and bulk purchases of $250,000 or more of similar items. Other property items, normal repairs, and maintenance are charged to expense as incurred. CFPB's established procedures for recording its property and equipment additions include that on a quarterly basis, the OCFO reviews property and equipment acquisitions and goods and services transactions of $50,000 and greater to help ensure that purchased items and costs associated with property and equipment, including internal-use software, are appropriately classified as capitalized assets or operating costs, consistent with its capitalization policy. For internal-use software, federal accounting standards provide that capitalized costs should include the full cost incurred during the software development stage, and exclude costs associated with preliminary design and post-implementation services.[9]

In our fiscal year 2013 audit opinion, we reported on a significant deficiency with respect to accounting for property and equipment.[10] Consequently, we separately reported the details of the significant deficiency, along with recommendations for corrective actions, in May 2014.[11] Based on these recommendations, with which it concurred, CFPB took actions in an attempt to improve the reporting of property and equipment. Such actions included the OCFO (1) working in conjunction with the Office of Procurement through monthly roundtable meetings to discuss financial-related topics and (2) performing additional reviews and analytics of contracts and interagency agreements for items that may meet the CFPB capitalization threshold.

However, the results of our fiscal year 2014 testing showed that CFPB continued to make errors in capitalizing costs and the OCFO's review was not effective in detecting and correcting these errors. Specifically, the results of our tests, which covered 100 percent of property and equipment additions in fiscal year 2014, revealed that CFPB erroneously capitalized as internal-use software and internal-use software in development $4.4 million in costs that related to maintenance and other operating costs that should have been included in gross cost. These errors occurred, in part, as a result of CFPB not having an effective mechanism to track the development stage for internal-use software. While the OCFO uses tracking schedules prepared by the applicable CORs and program offices to determine the current stage of internal-use software, these schedules change frequently and thus might be outdated at the time of capitalization. Consequently, CFPB cannot effectively determine whether the amounts invoiced represent costs associated with preliminary design, which should be expensed; software development, which should be capitalized; or post-implementation services, which should be expensed. We also found that the OCFO's quarterly reviews were not effective in detecting and correcting these errors to ensure that the amounts recorded for property and equipment were

---

[9]Statement of Federal Financial Accounting Standards No. 10, *Accounting for Internal Use Software*, October 9, 1998, as amended through June 30, 2014.

[10]GAO-14-170R.

[11]GAO-14-455R.

accurate and complete. For example, we found instances in which the invoices were not properly reviewed to determine whether the goods and services charged met the capitalization criteria. After we brought these issues to CFPB's attention, CFPB made the corresponding corrections to its fiscal year 2014 financial statements.

These deficiencies increase the risk that CFPB's reported balances for property and equipment as well as its reported expenses could be misstated, and collectively represent a significant deficiency in CFPB's internal control over its accounting for property and equipment that merits attention by those charged with governance. Until CFPB strengthens its control procedures to ensure (1) adequate and continuous coordination between the OCFO, CORs, the Office of Procurement, and other program offices at the time of capitalization and (2) effective review of property and equipment costs, the deficiencies in internal control over the accounting for property and equipment are likely to continue to exist.

Other Matters

Required Supplementary Information

U.S. generally accepted accounting principles issued by the Federal Accounting Standards Advisory Board (FASAB) require that the RSI be presented to supplement the financial statements. Although not a part of the financial statements, FASAB considers this information to be an essential part of financial reporting for placing the financial statements in appropriate operational, economic, or historical context. We have applied certain limited procedures to the RSI in accordance with U.S. generally accepted government auditing standards, which consisted of inquiries of management about the methods of preparing the RSI and comparing the information for consistency with management's responses to the auditor's inquiries, the financial statements, and other knowledge we obtained during the audit of the financial statements, in order to report omissions or material departures from FASAB guidelines, if any, identified by these limited procedures. We did not audit and we do not express an opinion or provide any assurance on the RSI because the limited procedures we applied do not provide sufficient evidence to express an opinion or provide any assurance.

Other Information

CFPB's other information contains information, some of which is not directly related to the financial statements. This information is presented for purposes of additional analysis and is not a required part of the financial statements or the RSI. We read the other information included with the financial statements in order to identify material inconsistencies, if any, with the audited financial statements. Our audit was conducted for the purpose of forming an opinion on CFPB's financial statements. We did not audit and do not express an opinion or provide any assurance on the other information.

Report on Compliance with Laws, Regulations, Contracts, and Grant Agreements

In connection with our audits of CFPB's financial statements, we tested compliance with selected provisions of applicable laws, regulations, contracts, and grant agreements consistent with the auditor's responsibility discussed below. We caution that noncompliance may occur and not be detected by these tests. We performed our tests of compliance in accordance with U.S. generally accepted government auditing standards.

Management's Responsibility

CFPB management is responsible for complying with laws, regulations, contracts, and grant agreements applicable to CFPB.

Auditor's Responsibility

Our responsibility is to test compliance with selected provisions of laws, regulations, contracts, and grant agreements applicable to CFPB that have a direct effect on the determination of material amounts and disclosures in the CFPB financial statements, and perform certain other limited procedures. Accordingly, we did not test compliance with all laws, regulations, contracts, and grant agreements applicable to CFPB.

Results of Our Tests for Compliance with Laws, Regulations, Contracts, and Grant Agreements

Our tests for compliance with selected provisions of applicable laws, regulations, contracts, and grant agreements disclosed no instances of noncompliance for fiscal year 2014 that would be reportable under U.S. generally accepted government auditing standards. However, the objective of our tests was not to provide an opinion on compliance with laws, regulations, contracts, and grant agreements applicable to CFPB. Accordingly, we do not express such an opinion.

Intended Purpose of Report on Compliance with Laws, Regulations, Contracts, and Grant Agreements

The purpose of this report is solely to describe the scope of our testing of compliance with selected provisions of applicable laws, regulations, contracts, and grant agreements, and the results of that testing, and not to provide an opinion on compliance. This report is an integral part of an audit performed in accordance with U.S. generally accepted government auditing standards in considering compliance. Accordingly, this report on compliance with laws, regulations, contracts, and grant agreements is not suitable for any other purpose.

Agency Comments

We provided a draft of this report to the Director of CFPB for comment. In his written comments, reprinted in appendix II, CFPB's Director stated that he was pleased to receive an unmodified audit opinion on the bureau's fiscal years 2014 and 2013 financial statements. The Director also agreed with the material weakness over reporting of accounts payable and the significant deficiency over accounting for property and equipment that we reported, and added that CFPB will continue to work to enhance its system of internal control and ensure the reliability of its financial reporting. The Director cited a number of steps CFPB plans to take in fiscal year 2015 to remediate these issues. Specifically, CFPB's plans for addressing the material weakness over reporting of accounts payable include completing and disseminating guidance for the CORs and invoice approvers; providing continuous and effective training to the CORs and invoice approvers; improving collaboration between the OCFO, CORs, and invoice approvers when calculating accrual amounts; increasing oversight of contracts and interagency agreements that affect accrual amounts; and performing more comprehensive review processes. To address the significant deficiency over accounting for property and equipment, CFPB stated that it plans to increase collaboration between the OCFO, CORs, invoice approvers, and the Office of Procurement; continue its review of contracts and interagency agreements; and implement a process to more systematically gather and disseminate information on fixed asset acquisitions to ensure that capitalized costs are accurately captured and recorded.

We will evaluate CFPB's actions to address the deficiencies identified in this report as part of our fiscal year 2015 audit.

J. Lawrence Malenich

J. Lawrence Malenich
Director
Financial Management and Assurance

November 10, 2014

Appendix I. Management's report on internal control over financial reporting

November 10, 2014

Mr. Gene Dodaro
Comptroller General of the United States
441 G Street, NW Washington, DC 20548

Dear Mr. Dodaro,

As required by Section 1017 of the Dodd-Frank Act, 12 U.S.C. Section 5497(a)(4)(D), the Consumer Financial Protection Bureau (CFPB) provides this management assertion regarding the effectiveness of internal control that apply to financial reporting by the CFPB based on criteria established in Section 3512(c) of Title 31, United States Code (commonly known as the Federal Managers' Financial Integrity Act) and applicable sections of Office of Management and Budget Circular A-123.

The CFPB's internal control over financial reporting is a process effected by those charged with governance, management, and other personnel, the objectives of which are to provide reasonable assurance that (1) transactions are properly recorded, processed, and summarized to permit the preparation of financial statements in accordance with U.S. generally accepted accounting principles, and assets are safeguarded against loss from unauthorized acquisition, use, or disposition; and (2) transactions are executed in accordance with laws governing the use of budget authority and with other applicable laws, regulations, contracts, and grant agreements that could have a direct and material effect on the financial statements.

CFPB management is responsible for maintaining effective internal control over financial reporting, including the design, implementation, and maintenance of internal control relevant to the preparation and fair presentation of financial statements that are free from material misstatement, whether due to fraud or error. CFPB management evaluated the effectiveness of CFPB's internal control over financial reporting as of September 30, 2014, based on the criteria established under 31 U.S.C. 3512(c) and applicable sections of Office of Management and Budget Circular A-123.

Based on the results of this evaluation, other than the material weakness identified regarding the accounts payable accruals process, as of September 30, 2014, the CFPB's internal control over financial reporting was operating effectively and no other material weaknesses were found in the design or operation of the internal control.

Richard Cordray

Richard Cordray
Director
Consumer Financial Protection Bureau

Stephen J. Agostini

Stephen J. Agostini
Chief Financial Officer
Consumer Financial Protection Bureau

Appendix II. Management's response to the auditor's report

November 12, 2014

Mr. J. Lawrence Malenich
Director, Financial Management and Assurance
Government Accountability Office
441 G Street, N.W., Room 5T45
Washington, DC 20548

Dear Mr. Malenich,

I appreciate the opportunity to respond to the Government Accountability Office's (GAO) draft audit report titled, Financial Audit: Bureau of Consumer Financial Protection's Fiscal Years 2014 and 2013 Financial Statements, and want to thank you and your staff for your dedicated efforts and collaboration to meet the audit requirements.

We are pleased that GAO's auditors rendered an unmodified or "clean" audit opinion, meaning GAO found that the Consumer Financial Protection Bureau (CFPB or Bureau) financial statements are presented fairly, in all material respects, and in conformity with U.S. generally accepted accounting principles, and that there were no instances of reportable noncompliance with laws and regulations tested by GAO. Maintaining an unmodified or "clean" audit opinion on the CFPB's comparative financial statements for fiscal years 2014 and 2013 is a significant accomplishment.

We acknowledge and concur with GAO's identification of one material weakness in internal control over the reporting of accounts payable. It is our understanding that this material weakness does not indicate that the Bureau overspent its funds in fiscal year 2014 (in fact it appears to have underspent them). Nevertheless, the Bureau is committed to correcting the imprecision in the accrual estimation process to ensure the proper accounting and reporting of the Bureau's expenses. In fiscal year 2013, a significant deficiency was identified in the accounts payable accrual process. During fiscal year 2014, the OCFO implemented corrective actions to mitigate the risks of this deficiency: provided additional outreach and guidance to Contracting Officer Representatives (COR) and invoice approvers, implemented a sampling methodology to review the accrual amounts, and began developing a resource and desk guide for the CORs and invoice approvers. The corrective actions implemented did not mitigate the risks appropriately and the errors in the accounts payable accrual amounts resulted in the identification of a material weakness. During fiscal year 2015, the Bureau will implement further steps to remediate these issues working with CORs, invoice approvers, and the Bureau's accountable officials. These corrective actions will include the completion and dissemination of the resource and desk guide for the CORs and invoice approvers, continuous and effective training for the CORs and invoice approvers, improved collaboration between the OCFO and the CORs and invoice approvers when calculating the accrual amounts, increased oversight by the OCFO over the budget execution of contracts and interagency agreements that impact the associated accrual amounts, and a more comprehensive OCFO review process over the accrual amounts.

In fiscal year 2014, the GAO cited one repeat significant deficiency regarding property and equipment. As a result of this significant deficiency identified in fiscal year 2013, during fiscal year 2014 the OCFO implemented corrective actions: provided additional outreach and guidance to CORs and invoice approvers and implemented a review process over contracts and interagency agreements for the purchase or development of items that may be capitalized. The corrective actions implemented did not fully mitigate the risks and therefore this significant deficiency is still identified in fiscal year 2014. During fiscal year 2015, the Bureau will increase its collaboration between the OCFO, applicable CORs and invoice approvers, and the Office of Procurement; continue its review over contracts and interagency agreements; and implement a process to more systematically gather and disseminate information on fixed asset acquisitions to ensure capitalized costs are accurately captured and recorded.

The CFPB will continue to work to enhance our system of internal control and ensure the reliability of CFPB's financial reporting. The CFPB looks forward to working with GAO in future audits and truly appreciates GAO's work over the past fiscal year.

If you have any questions relating to this response, please contact Stephen J. Agostini, Chief Financial Officer.

Richard Cordray

Richard Cordray
Director
Consumer Financial Protection Bureau

2.2 Financial statements and notes

CONSUMER FINANCIAL PROTECTION BUREAU
BALANCE SHEET
As of September 30, 2014 and 2013
(In Dollars)

	2014	2013
Assets:		
Intragovernmental		
Fund Balance with Treasury (Note 2)	$ 39,658,210	$ 26,764,046
Investments (Note 3)	434,793,473	343,797,086
Advances and Prepayments (Note 7)	2,900,006	4,993,642
Total Intragovernmental	477,351,689	375,554,774
Cash, and Other Monetary Assets		
Cash in the Bureau Fund (Note 4)	265,163	325,312
Cash in the Civil Penalty Fund (Note 4)	157,001,716	81,520,001
Total Cash, and Other Monetary Assets	157,266,879	81,845,313
Accounts Receivable (Note 5)	15,363,382	54,883
Property, Equipment, and Software, Net (Note 6)	37,496,598	27,684,477
Advances and Prepayments (Note 7)	2,706	749,699
Total Assets	$ 687,481,254	$ 485,889,146
Liabilities:		
Intragovernmental		
Accounts Payable	$ 27,209,775	$ 12,778,174
Benefits Payable	12,094,603	6,570,070
Other (Note 8)	442,000	270,811
Total Intragovernmental	39,746,378	19,619,055
Accounts Payable	28,713,030	19,400,933
Employer Benefits Contributions	29,658,237	11,131,319
Accrued Funded Payroll	4,553,007	3,441,835
Civil Penalty Fund Allocation (Note 4)	30,334,602	13,046,046
Unfunded Leave	16,400,954	11,939,809
Other (Note 8)	14,172	864
Total Liabilities (Note 9)	$ 149,420,380	$ 78,579,861
Commitments and Contingencies (Note 10)		
Net Position:		
Cumulative Results of Operations - Funds from Dedicated Collections (consolidated totals) (Note 17)	$ 538,060,874	$ 407,309,285
Total Liabilities and Net Position	$ 687,481,254	$ 485,889,146

The accompanying notes are an integral part of these financial statements.

CONSUMER FINANCIAL PROTECTION BUREAU
STATEMENT OF NET COST
For the Fiscal Years Ended September 30, 2014 and 2013
(In Dollars)

	2014	2013
Program Costs:		
Prevent Financial Harm to Consumers While Promoting Good Practices That Benefit Them:		
Gross Costs	$ 228,378,527	$ 166,120,841
Net Prevent Financial Harm to Consumers While Promoting Good Practices That Benefit Them	$ 228,378,527	$ 166,120,841
Empower Consumers to Live Better Financial Lives:		
Gross Costs	$ 100,716,666	$ 70,921,575
Net Empower Consumers to Live Better Financial Lives	$ 100,716,666	$ 70,921,575
Inform The Public, Policy Makers, and the CFPB's own Policy-Making with Data-Driven Analysis of Consumer Finance Markets and Consumer Behavior:		
Gross Costs	$ 45,763,864	$ 43,144,983
Less: Earned Revenue	(80,000)	
Net Inform The Public, Policy Makers, and the CFPB's own Policy-Making with Data-Driven Analysis of Consumer Finance Markets and Consumer Behavior	$ 45,683,864	$ 43,144,983
Advance the CFPB's Performance by Maximizing Resource Productivity & Enhancing Impact:		
Gross Costs	$ 122,774,691	$ 111,137,443
Net Advance the CFPB's Performance by Maximizing Resource Productivity & Enhancing Impact	$ 122,774,691	$ 111,137,443
Total Gross Program Costs	$ 497,633,748	$ 391,324,842
Less: Total Earned Revenues	$ (80,000)	
Net Cost of Operations (Note 11)	$ 497,553,748	$ 391,324,842

The accompanying notes are an integral part of these financial statements.

CONSUMER FINANCIAL PROTECTION BUREAU
STATEMENT OF CHANGES IN NET POSITION
For the Fiscal Years Ended September 30, 2014 and 2013
(In Dollars)

	2014	2013
Cumulative Results of Operations:		
Beginning Balances	$ 407,309,285	$ 228,503,943
Budgetary Financing Sources:		
Nonexchange Revenue		
Transfers from the Board of Governors of the Federal Reserve System	533,800,000	518,400,000
Civil Penalties	92,702,001	49,520,001
Interstate Land Sales Fees	149,600	146,900
Interest from Investments	132,368	204,345
Total Nonexchange Revenue	626,783,969	568,271,246
Other	3,870	10,089
Other Financing Sources (Non-Exchange):		
Imputed Financing Sources	1,517,498	1,848,849
Total Financing Sources	628,305,337	570,130,184
Net Cost of Operations	(497,553,748)	(391,324,842)
Net Change	130,751,589	178,805,342
Cumulative Results of Operations - Funds from Dedicated Collections (consolidated totals) (Note 17)	$ 538,060,874	$ 407,309,285
Net Position	$ 538,060,874	$ 407,309,285

The accompanying notes are an integral part of these financial statements.

CONSUMER FINANCIAL PROTECTION BUREAU
STATEMENT OF BUDGETARY RESOURCES
For the Fiscal Years Ended September 30, 2014 and 2013
(In Dollars)

	2014	2013
Budgetary Resources:		
Unobligated Balance Brought Forward, October 1	$ 169,931,592	$ 131,568,070
Recoveries of Prior Year Unpaid Obligations	14,992,113	8,750,005
Unobligated Balance from Prior Year Budget Authority, Net	184,923,705	140,318,075
Funds Available for Obligation	611,594,848	568,288,019
Spending Authority from Offsetting Collections	199,932	84,614
Total Budgetary Resources	$ 796,718,485	$ 708,690,708
Status of Budgetary Resources:		
Obligations Incurred (Note 12)	$ 499,812,046	$ 538,759,116
Unobligated Balance, End of Year:		
Exempt from Apportionment	296,906,439	169,931,592
Total Budgetary Resources	$ 796,718,485	$ 708,690,708
Change in Obligated Balance:		
Unpaid Obligations:		
Unpaid Obligations, Brought Forward, October 1	$ 282,450,772	$ 109,033,128
Obligations Incurred	499,812,046	538,759,116
Outlays (Gross)	(432,475,653)	(356,591,467)
Recoveries of Prior Year Unpaid Obligations	(14,992,113)	(8,750,005)
Unpaid Obligations, End of Year	$ 334,795,052	$ 282,450,772
Memorandum (non-add) Entries:		
Obligated Balance, Start of Year	$ 282,450,772	$ 109,033,128
Obligated Balance, End of Year	$ 334,795,052	$ 282,450,772
Budget Authority and Outlays, Net:		
Budget Authority, Gross	$ 611,794,780	$ 568,372,633
Actual Offsetting Collections	(199,932)	(84,614)
Budget Authority, Net	$ 611,594,848	$ 568,288,019
Outlays, Gross	$ 432,475,653	$ 356,591,467
Actual Offsetting Collections	(199,932)	(84,614)
Agency Outlays, Net	$ 432,275,721	$ 356,506,853

The accompanying notes are an integral part of these financial statements.

CONSUMER FINANCIAL PROTECTION BUREAU
STATEMENT OF CUSTODIAL ACTIVITY
For the Fiscal Years Ended September 30, 2014 and 2013
(In Dollars)

	2014	2013
Revenue Activity:		
Sources of Cash Collections:		
Disgorgement	$ 27,076	$ 118,194
Miscellaneous	20,002	3,369
Total Cash Collections	47,078	121,563
Accrual Adjustments	(1,384)	6,638
Total Custodial Revenue	45,694	128,201
Disposition of Collections:		
Amounts Transferred to the Department of the Treasury	47,078	121,563
Increase/(Decrease) in Amounts Yet to be Transferred	(1,384)	6,638
Net Custodial Activity	$ -	$ -

The accompanying notes are an integral part of these financial statements.

Note 1: Summary of significant accounting policies

A. Reporting entity

The Bureau of Consumer Financial Protection, known as the Consumer Financial Protection Bureau (CFPB), was established on July 21, 2010 under Title X of the Dodd-Frank Wall Street Reform and Consumer Protection Act Public Law No. 111-203 (Dodd-Frank Act). The CFPB was established as an independent bureau within the Federal Reserve System. The Bureau is an Executive agency as defined in section 105 of Title 5, United States Code. Section 1017 of the Dodd-Frank Act provides that the CFPB financial statements are not to be consolidated with the financial statements of either the Board of Governors of the Federal Reserve or the Federal Reserve System.

The Dodd-Frank Act authorizes the CFPB to exercise its authorities to ensure that, with respect to consumer financial products and services:

- a. Consumers are provided with timely and understandable information to make responsible decisions about financial transactions;
- b. Consumers are protected from unfair, deceptive, or abusive acts and practices and from discrimination;
- c. Outdated, unnecessary, or unduly burdensome regulations are regularly identified and addressed in order to reduce unwarranted regulatory burdens;
- d. Federal consumer financial law is enforced consistently in order to promote fair competition; and
- e. Markets for consumer financial products and services operate transparently and efficiently to facilitate access and innovation.

Under the Dodd-Frank Act, on the designated transfer date, July 21, 2011, certain authorities and functions of several agencies relating to Federal consumer financial law were transferred to the CFPB in order to accomplish the above objectives. These authorities were transferred from the Board of Governors of the Federal Reserve System (Board of Governors), Comptroller of the Currency (OCC), Office of Thrift Supervision (OTS), Federal Deposit Insurance Corporation (FDIC), National Credit Union Administration (NCUA), and the Department of Housing and Urban Development (HUD). In addition, Congress vested the Bureau with authority to enforce in certain circumstances the Federal Trade Commission's (FTC) Telemarketing Sales Rule and its rules under the FTC Act, although the FTC retains full authority over these rules. The Dodd-Frank Act also provided the CFPB with certain other federal consumer financial regulatory authorities in addition to these transferred authorities.

To accomplish its mission, the CFPB is organized into six primary divisions/offices:

1. **Consumer Education and Engagement:** provides, through a variety of initiatives and methods, including offices on specific populations, information to consumers to allow them to make financial decisions that are best for them.

2. **Supervision, Enforcement and Fair Lending:** ensures compliance with Federal consumer financial laws by supervising market participants and bringing enforcement actions when appropriate.

3. **Research, Markets and Regulations:** conducts research to understand consumer financial markets and consumer behavior, evaluates whether there is a need for regulation, and determines the costs and benefits of potential or existing regulations.

4. **Legal Division:** ensures the Bureau's compliance with all applicable laws and provides advice to the Director and the Bureau's divisions.

5. **External Affairs:** manages the Bureau's relationships with external stakeholders and ensures that the Bureau maintains robust dialogue with interested stakeholders to promote understanding, transparency, and accountability.

6. **Operations:** builds and sustains the CFPB's operational infrastructure to support the entire organization and hears directly from consumers about challenges they face in the marketplaces through their complaints, questions, and feedback.

The CFPB workforce is spread across the country with its headquarters in Washington, D.C. and regional offices in Chicago, New York City, and San Francisco. The headquarters is temporarily spread across several locations within Washington, D.C., utilizing space pursuant to interagency agreements with the Department of the Treasury (Treasury), the Office of the Comptroller of the Currency, the General Services Administration (GSA) and the Federal Housing Finance Agency (FHFA). In addition to its locations within Washington D.C., the CFPB also utilizes space pursuant to occupancy agreements with GSA for the regional offices in New York, Chicago and San Francisco.

Additional information on the organizational structure and responsibilities of CFPB is available on CFPB's website at http://www.consumerfinance.gov/.

B. Basis of presentation

The CFPB's principal statements were prepared from its official financial records and general ledger in conformity with U.S. generally accepted accounting principles (GAAP) and, while not required to comply with all OMB guidance such as OMB Circular A-136, CFPB generally tracks the general presentation guidance established by OMB Circular A-136, *Financial Reporting Requirements,* as revised. The financial statements are a requirement of the Dodd-Frank Act. The financial statements are in addition to the financial reports prepared by the CFPB, which are used to monitor and control budgetary resources. The financial statements have been prepared to report the financial position, net cost of operations, changes in net position, the status and availability of budgetary resources, and the custodial activities of the CFPB. Financial statements are presented on a comparative basis. During fiscal year 2013, the CFPB prepared and issued a strategic plan that contains four strategic goals and associated performance metrics. The strategic plan was designed to meet the objectives of the Government Performance and Results Act and help the CFPB measure its performance in fulfilling its responsibilities under the Dodd-Frank Act. The comparative statement of net cost contains four responsibility segments based on the strategic plan.

C. Basis of accounting

Transactions are recorded on both an accrual accounting basis and a budgetary basis. Under the accrual basis of accounting, revenues are recognized when earned, and expenses are recognized when a liability is incurred, without regard to receipt or payment of cash. Budgetary accounting facilitates compliance with legal requirements and controls over the use of funds. The Statement of Custodial Activity is presented on the modified cash basis of accounting. Cash collections and amounts transferred to Treasury are reported on a cash basis. The change in receivables is reported on an accrual basis. The CFPB conforms to GAAP for federal entities as prescribed by the standards set forth by the Federal Accounting Standards Advisory Board (FASAB). FASAB is recognized by the American Institute of Certified Public Accountants as the body designated to establish GAAP for federal government entities. Certain assets, liabilities and costs have been classified as intragovernmental throughout the financial statements and notes. Intragovernmental assets and liabilities are those due from or to other federal entities. Intragovernmental costs are payments or accruals due to other federal entities. The CFPB has rights and ownership of all assets, except for custodial assets, reported in these financial statements. Custodial/Non-entity assets can result from CFPB enforcement actions that require the defendant to pay disgorgement as well as from the collection of Freedom of Information Act fees. Disgorgement is an equitable remedy that a court or the CFPB can impose in a judicial or administrative action to deprive defendants of their ill-gotten gains and to deter violations of Federal consumer financial laws. In addition, as further discussed in Note 1.R. and Note 19, the CFPB also administers certain funds in a fiduciary capacity.

D. Funding sources

The CFPB's funding is obtained primarily through transfers from the Board of Governors, interest earned on investments, and penalties and fees collected. The Dodd-Frank Act requires the CFPB to maintain an account with the Federal Reserve – the "Bureau of Consumer Financial Protection Fund" (Bureau Fund). The Director of the CFPB, or his designee, requests transfers from the Board of Governors in amounts necessary to carry out the authorities and operations of the Bureau. The Board of Governors transfers the funds into the Bureau Fund, which is maintained at the Federal Reserve Bank of New York (FRBNY). Bureau funds determined not needed to meet the current needs of the Bureau are invested in Treasury securities on the open market. Earnings from the investments are also deposited into this fund. The CFPB requests funds on a quarterly basis. The funds maintained at the FRBNY are reported in the financial statements and related notes and represent budget authority for CFPB.

The CFPB funding requests for the Bureau Fund are capped as follows:

The amount that shall be transferred to the Bureau in each fiscal year shall not exceed a fixed percentage of the total operating expenses ($4.98 billion) of the Federal Reserve System, subject to an annual inflation adjustment, as reported in the Annual Report, 2009, of the Board of Governors, equal to:

- In fiscal year 2011, up to 10 percent of these Federal Reserve System expenses (or approximately $498 million),
- In fiscal year 2012, up to 11 percent of these expenses (or approximately $547.8 million),

- In fiscal year 2013, up to 12 percent of these expenses (or approximately $597.6 million), and

- In fiscal year 2014 and beyond, the cap remains at 12 percent but will be adjusted annually based on the percentage increase in the employment cost index for total compensation for State and local government workers published by the Federal Government.

The Dodd-Frank Act explicitly provides that Bureau funds obtained by or transferred to the Bureau Fund are not Government funds or appropriated funds.

If the Director were to determine that the non-appropriated funds to which it is entitled under the Act are insufficient to carry out its responsibilities, the Act provided the potential for the CFPB also to obtain appropriated funds, up to a capped amount, in fiscal years 2011-2014. There has been no such determination. In accordance with the Act and appropriations law requirements, further action would have been required on the part of the Director and Congress in order for CFPB to obtain such appropriated funds.

The CFPB also collects filing fees from developers under the Interstate Land Sales Full Disclosure Act (ILSA). ILSA protects consumers from fraud and abuse in the sale or lease of land. On July 21, 2011, the responsibility for administering ILSA was transferred to the CFPB from HUD pursuant to the Dodd-Frank Act. The Dodd-Frank Act requires land developers to register subdivisions of 100 or more non-exempt lots and to provide each purchaser with a disclosure document called a Property Report. Developers must pay a fee when they register such subdivisions. While the CFPB continues to administer the legislation with respect to the transfer of these functions under the ILSA, and collect the fees, the fees are currently being deposited into an account maintained by Treasury. The fees collected may be retained and are available until expended for the purpose of covering all or part of the costs that the Bureau incurs for ILSA program operations.

Pursuant to the Dodd-Frank Act, the CFPB is also authorized to obtain civil penalties for violations of Federal consumer financial laws. The Act requires the CFPB to maintain a separate fund, known as the Consumer Financial Civil Penalty Fund (Civil Penalty Fund). Civil penalties are deposited into the Civil Penalty Fund established and maintained at the FRBNY. The Act authorizes the CFPB to use the Civil Penalty Fund for payment to the victims of activities for which civil penalties have been imposed and, in certain circumstances, for consumer education and financial literacy programs. Amounts in the Civil Penalty Fund are available "without fiscal year limitation." The Civil Penalty Fund had its initial collections and deposits in fiscal year 2012.

The CFPB also recognizes imputed financing sources. An imputed financing source is recognized by the receiving entity for costs that are paid by other entities. The CFPB recognized imputed costs and financing sources in fiscal years 2014 and 2013 as prescribed by accounting standards. The CFPB recognizes as an imputed financing source the amount of pension and post-retirement benefit expenses for current employees that OCC and the Office of Personnel Management (OPM) has or will pay on the CFPB's behalf. Further, CFPB recognized earned revenue for reimbursable activity of CFPB staff detailed to an educational institution for conducting research.

E. Use of estimates

The Bureau has made certain estimates and assumptions relating to the reporting of assets, liabilities, revenues, expenses, and the disclosure of contingent liabilities to prepare these financial statements. The estimates are based on current conditions that may change in the future. Actual results could differ from these estimates. Some of the significant transactions subject to estimates include costs regarding benefit plans for the CFPB employees that are administered by OPM, OCC and the Federal Reserve System, costs regarding payments to victims from the Civil Penalty Fund, and cost allocations among the programs on the Statement of Net Cost.

F. Funds from dedicated collections

FASAB's Statement of Federal Financial Accounting Standards (SFFAS) No. 27 "Identifying and Reporting Earmarked Funds" established certain disclosure requirements for funds defined as "earmarked." In June 2012, FASAB issued SFFAS 43, *Funds from Dedicated Collections: Amending Statement of Federal Financial Accounting Standards 27, Identifying and Reporting Earmarked Funds.* SFFAS 43 amendments include changing the term "earmarked funds" to "funds from dedicated collections." SFFAS 27, as amended by SFFAS 43, contains three requirements for funds to be considered funds from dedicated collection: (1) A statute committing the federal government to use specifically identified revenues and/or other financing sources that are originally provided to the federal government by a non-federal source only for designated activities, benefits or purposes; (2) Explicit authority for the fund to retain revenues and/or other financing sources not used in the current period for future use to finance the designated activities, benefits, or purposes; and (3) A requirement to account for and report on the receipt, use and retention of the revenues and/or other financing sources that distinguishes the fund from the federal government's general revenues.

Based on the standard's criteria, CFPB has determined that the Bureau Fund is a fund from dedicated collections due to its meeting the three required criteria – source of funds are from a non-federal source, explicit authority to retain funds for future use, and a requirement to account for and report on the funds receipt, use and retention separate from the federal government's general revenues. Further, the CFPB has determined based on the criteria of SFFAS 27 & 43 that the Civil Penalty Fund is also a fund from dedicated collections and has established a separate special fund to account for its activity. These funds, which also qualify as special funds, are discussed further in Note 1.H. below. SFFAS 43 is effective for fiscal year 2013 reporting beginning on October 1, 2012. Accordingly, the CFPB's comparative statements for fiscal years 2014 and 2013 are displayed consistent with the reporting requirements of SFFAS 27 & 43. See additional disclosure in Note 17 "Funds from Dedicated Collections."

G. Entity and non-entity assets

Entity assets are assets that the CFPB may use in its operations. This includes amounts where the CFPB management has the authority to decide how funds will be used. Non-Entity Assets are those assets that an agency holds on behalf of another Federal agency or on behalf of a third party and are not available for the agency's use. The CFPB's non-entity assets include cash from disgorgement payments made by defendants and collections from Freedom of Information Act fees as recorded in the Statement of Custodial Activity.

H. Fund balance with Treasury

The U.S. Treasury holds funds in the Treasury General Account for CFPB which are available to pay agency liabilities and to finance authorized purchase obligations. Treasury processes cash receipts, such as fees collected from the ILSA program, and makes disbursements on CFPB's behalf. As discussed in Note 1.D. above, CFPB also maintains an account with the FRBNY known as the Bureau Fund. During the year, increases to the Bureau Fund are generally comprised of fund transfers from the Board of Governors and investment interest. These funds are available for transfer to CFPB's Fund Balance with Treasury. Also, as discussed above in

Note 1.D., CFPB maintains an additional account at the FRBNY for the Civil Penalty Fund. These funds are also available for transfer to CFPB's Fund Balance with Treasury under a separate fund symbol from the Bureau Fund. CFPB's Fund Balance with Treasury for the activity described above is maintained in special funds. A special fund is established where the law requires collections to be used for a specific purpose, and the law neither authorizes the fund to conduct a cycle of business-type operations (making it a revolving fund) nor designates it as a trust fund.

CFPB also receives custodial revenues and fiduciary activity that are maintained in the Miscellaneous Receipts Fund of the U.S. Treasury, and a deposit fund respectively. The Miscellaneous Receipts fund holds non-entity receipts from custodial collections that the CFPB cannot deposit into funds under its control. This fund includes disgorgement deposits and any other miscellaneous funds collected (i.e., FOIA fees) that will be sent to the U.S. Treasury General Fund upon collection. Enforcement activity can result in CFPB receiving redress funds that are maintained in a deposit fund. Redress funds are held in a fiduciary capacity until CFPB can make payment directly to the harmed individuals or entities.

I. Investments

CFPB has the authority to invest the funds in the Bureau Fund account that are not required to meet the current needs of the Bureau. CFPB invests solely in U.S. Treasury securities purchased at a discount on the open market, which are normally held to maturity and carried at cost. CFPB selects investments with maturities suitable to its needs, currently three-month Treasury bills. Investments are adjusted for discounts. In accordance with GAAP, CFPB records the value of its investments in U.S. Treasury securities at cost and amortizes the discount on a straight-line basis over the term of the respective issues. Results under the straight line method approximate results under the interest method. Interest is credited to the Bureau Fund.

J. Accounts receivable

Accounts receivable consists of amounts owed to CFPB by the public. An allowance for uncollectible accounts receivable from the public is established when either (1) management determines that collection is unlikely to occur after a review of outstanding accounts and the failure of all collection efforts, or (2) an account for which no allowance has been established is submitted to Treasury for collection, which generally takes place when it becomes 120 days delinquent.

K. Property, Equipment, and Software, Net

Property, Equipment, and Software is recorded at historical cost. It consists of tangible assets and software. Under CFPB's property management policy, equipment acquisitions of $50,000 or more are capitalized and depreciated using the straight-line method (using a half year convention for the year assets are placed into service) over the estimated useful life of the asset. Similarly, internal use software, software purchased or developed to facilitate the operation of an entity's programs, is capitalized for software of $750,000 or more and depreciated using the straight-line method (using a half year convention) over the estimated useful life of the asset. Additionally, for bulk purchases of similar items, which individually do not meet the capitalization threshold, the acquisition is capitalized and depreciated if the depreciated basis of the bulk purchase is $250,000 or more. Applicable standard governmental guidelines regulate the disposal and convertibility of agency property and equipment.

The useful life classifications for capitalized assets are as follows:

PP&E Category	Useful Lives (years)
Laptop/Desktop Computers	3
Internal Use Software	5
Mainframe Computer System	7
Servers	7
Telecommunications Equipment	7
Furniture	8
Other Equipment	10

A leasehold (capital) improvement's useful life is equal to the remaining occupancy agreement term or the estimated useful life of the improvement, whichever is shorter. CFPB has no real property holdings or stewardship or heritage assets. Other property items, normal repairs, and maintenance are charged to expense as incurred.

L. Advances and Prepaid Charges

Advances and prepayments may occur as a result of reimbursable agreements, subscriptions, payments to contractors and employees, and payments to entities administering benefit programs for CFPB employees. Payments made in advance of the receipt of goods and services are recorded as advances or prepaid charges at the time of prepayment and recognized as expenses when the related goods and services are received.

M. Liabilities

Liabilities represent the amount of monies likely to be paid by CFPB as a result of transactions or events that have already occurred. Liabilities may be intragovernmental (claims against the CFPB by other Federal agencies) or with the public (claims against CFPB by an entity or person that is not a Federal agency). However, no liability can be paid if there is no funding. Liabilities for which funds are not available, therefore, are classified as not covered by budgetary resources. There is no certainty that the funding will be received. Additionally, the Government, acting in its sovereign capacity, can abrogate liabilities. Liabilities not covered by budgetary resources on the Balance Sheet are equivalent to amounts reported as components not requiring or generating resources on the Reconciliation of Net Cost to Budget.

CIVIL PENALTY FUND

The CFPB has determined that for the funds collected and deposited into the Civil Penalty Fund (CPF), victims do not have ownership rights to those funds that the Federal government must uphold. Accordingly, until CFPB decides to allocate CPF monies to classes of victims, no liabilities exist. The estimated amount of the liabilities of the Civil Penalty Fund will be recorded based on the results of the defined allocation process. The measurement of the liability will be based on the amount allocated by the Fund Administrator via the Civil Penalty Fund allocation process. The amount allocated by the Fund Administrator may differ from the amount of uncompensated harm initially estimated based on the court order, settlement agreement, or documentation provided by the Office of Enforcement. The allocated amount may differ based on additional research and documentation obtained after the initial estimate was calculated.

N. Annual, Sick, and Other Leave

Annual leave, compensatory time, and credit hours earned by the Bureau's employees, but not yet used, are reported as accrued liabilities. The accrued balance is adjusted annually to current pay rates. The accrued leave, for which funding is not available, is recorded as an unfunded liability. Sick and other leave are expensed as taken.

O. Employee Benefits

CFPB employees can elect to enroll in various benefit programs – medical, vision, dental, long-term disability, life insurance, etc.

BENEFITS FOR EMPLOYEES TRANSFERRED PURSUANT TO THE DODD-FRANK ACT

The Dodd-Frank Act provided employees transferred from other agencies (Board of Governors, Federal Reserve Banks, OCC, OTS, FDIC, NCUA, and HUD) with the ability to continue participation in the transferring agency or bank's non-Title 5 benefit programs for one year from the CFPB transfer date of July 21, 2011. The transferring agencies continued to administer the non-Title 5 benefit programs for those transferred employees continuing participation in the transferring agencies' plans for the one-year period. Upon conclusion of the one-year period, the employees had the opportunity to enroll in Title 5 benefit programs and/or in non-Title 5 benefit programs sponsored by CFPB. Title 5 of the U.S. Code outlines benefit programs for the majority of the Federal workforce, which are typically administered by OPM. For those employees participating in the transferring agencies' programs, CFPB reimbursed the transferring agencies for the employer's contribution to the programs. CFPB also has reimbursed the transferring agencies for administrative costs pursuant to memoranda of understanding with the transferring agencies. These costs are reflected as expenses in CFPB's financial statements.

BENEFITS FOR EMPLOYEES NOT TRANSFERRED PURSUANT TO THE DODD-FRANK ACT

Employees not transferred to the Bureau pursuant to the Dodd-Frank Act may enroll in some benefit programs administered by OPM and also have the option to enroll in non-Title 5 benefit programs sponsored by CFPB in addition to, or in lieu of, OPM programs. For those employees participating in OPM's benefit programs, CFPB records the employer's contribution to those programs. For those employees participating in CFPB's non-Title 5 benefit programs, CFPB directly contracts with vendors to provide those services. The Bureau recognizes the employer's contributions for these benefits as the benefits are earned. All of these costs are reflected as expenses in CFPB's financial statements.

P. Pension costs and other retirement benefits

CFPB employees are enrolled in several retirement and pension programs and post-employment benefits in accordance with the Dodd-Frank Act.

EMPLOYEES TRANSFERRED FROM THE FEDERAL RESERVE, OCC, OTS, FDIC, AND HUD
The Dodd-Frank Act allowed employees transferred from OCC, OTS, FDIC, and HUD to continue participating in the pension or retirement plans in which they were enrolled at their transferring agency or to affirmatively elect, between January 21, 2012 and January 20, 2013, to join the Federal Reserve System Retirement Plan and the Federal Reserve System Thrift Plan. Many transferee employees from these agencies are in the traditional Title 5 retirement plans (Federal Employees Retirement System (FERS), Civil Service Retirement System (CSRS), or CSRS Offset); however, a few transferees from OTS are in a non-Title 5 plan (i.e., Pentegra Defined Benefit Plan). Transferees from the Federal Reserve were allowed to remain in the Federal Reserve System retirement program or to affirmatively elect into the appropriate Title 5 retirement plan during that same timeframe. For those employees who elected to enroll in an alternative retirement plan, the enrollment became effective in January 2013.

CFPB does not report on its financial statements information pertaining to the retirement plans covering its employees. Reporting amounts such as plan assets, accumulated plan benefits, and related unfunded liabilities, if any, is the responsibility of the Federal Reserve System, OCC, or OPM as the administrator of their respective plans. In all cases, CFPB pays any employer contributions required by the plans. Refer to the chart below for information on which agency administers each of the retirement plans for CFPB employees.

OCC, OTS, and FDIC also offered other agency-only savings plans to employees. Any transferees who participated in such plans are allowed to continue their participation as long as they remain enrolled in their current retirement plans. In such cases, CFPB pays any employer contributions. Employees who elect to enroll in the Federal Reserve System retirement plan will not be allowed to continue their participation in either the Title 5 Thrift Savings Plan or the OCC, OTS, and FDIC agency savings plans.

CFPB has also reimbursed the transferring agencies for administrative costs pursuant to memoranda of understanding with the transferring agencies. These costs are reflected as expenses in CFPB's financial statements.

ALL OTHER EMPLOYEES OF CFPB

Employees hired with prior Title 5 Federal Retirement System coverage who are not transferees under the Dodd Frank Act may remain enrolled in the appropriate retirement programs administered by OPM – CSRS, CSRS Offset, or FERS. These employees alternatively have the option to enroll in the Federal Reserve System retirement plans. CFPB began providing these new employees the opportunity to enroll in the Federal Reserve retirement system plans beginning in November 2011. For those employees electing to enroll in the Federal Reserve System's retirement plans, the enrollment becomes effective at the beginning of the pay period following receipt of their written election decision. New employees with no previous coverage under a Title 5 retirement plan are automatically enrolled in the Federal Reserve System's retirement plans. CFPB pays the employer's contribution into those plans.

TABLE 28: PENSION/RETIREMENT PLANS FOR CFPB EMPLOYEES

Name	Administering Agency
Federal Reserve System Retirement Plan (FRSRP)	Federal Reserve System
Federal Reserve System Thrift Plan	Federal Reserve System
Pension Enhancement Plan for Officers of the Board of Governors of the Federal Reserve System	Federal Reserve System
Retirement Plan for Employees of the Federal Reserve System Benefits Equalization Plan[1]	Federal Reserve System
Retirement Plan for Employees of the Federal Reserve System Benefits Equalization Plan for Section 415 Excess Benefits	Federal Reserve System
Thrift Plan for Employees of the Federal Reserve System Benefits Equalization Plan[1]	Federal Reserve System
Civil Service Retirement System (CSRS)	OPM
CSRS Offset	OPM
Federal Employees Retirement System (FERS)	OPM

Thrift Savings Plan	Federal Retirement Thrift Investment Board
FDIC Savings Plan	FDIC
OCC 401(k)	OCC
OTS 401(k)	OCC
OTS Deferred Compensation Plan	OCC
Pentegra Defined Benefit Plan (OTS)	OCC (administration is through Pentegra)

[1] This retirement program does not have any CFPB participants for fiscal years 2013 or 2014.

The Bureau does not have a separate pension or retirement plan distinct from the plans described above. CFPB expenses its contributions to the retirement plans of covered employees as the expenses are incurred. CFPB reported imputed costs (not paid by CFPB) with respect to retirement plans (OPM-administered), health benefits and life insurance (for employees retiring under Title 5 retirement plans; OPM-administered) pursuant to guidance received from OPM. These costs are paid by OPM. Disclosure is intended to provide information regarding the full cost of CFPB's program in conformity with GAAP. CFPB, however, records expenses for the post-retirement health benefits (i.e., health benefits also OPM-administered) for those employees retiring under the Federal Reserve System retirement plans. These costs are not imputed costs with OPM. The associated liabilities for these post-retirement health benefits are incorporated as part of the line item on the Balance Sheet for Benefits Payable.

The Bureau recognizes the employer's contributions for the retirement plans administered by the Federal Reserve. The Bureau is responsible for transferring to the Federal Reserve both the employer's contributions and the employee's contributions that the Bureau has collected from employees. Under section 1013(a)(3)(C) of the Dodd-Frank Act, CFPB is required to pay an employer contribution to the FRSRP in an amount established by the employer contribution under the Federal Employees Retirement System – currently 11.9 percent of salary. For fiscal years 2014 and 2013 those amounts were $16.9 and $13.1 million, respectively.

Consistent with the disclosures in the financial statements of the Board of Governors of the Federal Reserve System, the FRSRP provides retirement benefits to employees of the Board, the Reserve Banks and certain employees of the CFPB. The FRBNY, on behalf of the Federal Reserve System, recognizes the net assets and costs associated with the System Plan in its financial statements. Consistent with provisions of a single-employer plan, costs associated with the System Plan are aggregated by the FRBNY on behalf of the Federal Reserve Systems and were not redistributed to individual entities (e.g., CFPB). Accordingly, the CFPB cannot report the full cost of the plan benefits applicable to CFPB employees. Please see the Federal Reserve Banks Combined Financial Statements for the net assets and costs associated with the System Plan (www.federalreserve.gov/publications/annual-report/files/2013-annual-report.pdf).

Q. Commitments and Contingencies

A commitment is a preliminary action that reserves available funds until an obligation is made which will result in a legal liability of the U.S. government. Examples of a commitment include purchase requisitions or unsigned contracts. All open commitments at year end are closed out and new commitments (requisitions) need to be recorded in the next fiscal year. Accordingly, no open commitments exist at year end to report in the either the financial statements or notes.

Liabilities are deemed contingent when the existence or amount of the liability cannot be determined with certainty pending the outcome of future events. Contingencies are recognized on the balance sheet and statement of net cost when the liability is probable and can be reasonably estimated. Contingencies are disclosed in the notes to the financial statements when there is a reasonable possibility of a loss from the outcome of future events or when there is a probable loss that cannot be reasonably estimated. See Note 10 for additional information.

R. Fiduciary activities

The Dodd-Frank Act, section 1055 authorizes the court in a judicial action or the CFPB in an administrative proceeding to grant any appropriate legal or equitable relief for a violation of Federal consumer financial law. Such relief may include redress for victims of the violations, including refunds, restitution, and damages. Relief that is intended to compensate victims is treated as fiduciary funds and deposited into the "Legal or Equitable Relief Fund" established at the Department of the Treasury. Fiduciary assets are not assets of the CFPB and are not recognized on the balance sheet. See Note 19, Fiduciary Activities.

S. Custodial activities

Under section 1055 of the Dodd-Frank Act, the CFPB may obtain disgorgement for violations of Federal consumer law. Disgorgement paid by the defendant is treated by CFPB as a custodial activity. CFPB will report those disgorged deposits and any other miscellaneous funds collected (i.e., FOIA fees) on the Statement of Custodial Activity.

Note 2: Fund balance with Treasury

Fund Balance with Treasury account balances as of September 30, 2014 and September 30, 2013 were as follows:

	2014	2013
Fund Balances:		
Special Fund	$ 39,658,210	$ 26,764,046
Total	$ 39,658,210	$ 26,764,046
Status of Fund Balance with Treasury:		
Unobligated Balance		
Available	$ 296,906,439	$ 169,931,592
Obligated Balance Not Yet Disbursed	334,795,052	282,450,772
Investments at Cost	(434,776,402)	(343,773,005)
Cash Held Outside of Treasury (See Note 4)	(157,266,879)	(81,845,313)
Total	$ 39,658,210	$ 26,764,046

Unobligated Balance Available represents the amount of budget authority that can be used to enter into new obligations. This amount, or a portion thereof, may be administratively dedicated for specific purposes that have not yet been obligated. The Obligated Balance Not Yet Disbursed represents amounts designated for payment of goods and services ordered but not received or goods and services received but for which payment has not yet been made.

Note 3: Investments

As discussed further in Note 4, at the direction of the CFPB, the FRBNY invests the portion of the Bureau Fund that is not required to meet the current needs of the Bureau. When directed by CFPB, the FRBNY will utilize the funds available to purchase investments on the open market. At this time, CFPB only invests in three month U.S. Treasury bills. The market value is determined by the secondary U.S. Treasury market and represents the value an individual investor is willing to pay for these securities, as of September 30, 2014 and September 30, 2013.

Investments as of September 30, 2014 consist of the following:

	Cost	Amortization Method	Amortized Discount	Investments Net	Market Value Disclosure
Intragovernmental Securities:					
Marketable	434,776,402	Straight-Line	17,071	434,793,473	434,794,302
Total	$434,776,402		$17,071	$434,793,473	$434,794,302

Investments as of September 30, 2013 consist of the following:

	Cost	Amortization Method	Amortized Discount	Investments Net	Market Value Disclosure
Intragovernmental Securities:					
Marketable	343,773,005	Straight-Line	24,081	343,797,086	343,797,757
Total	$343,773,005		$24,081	$343,797,086	$343,797,757

Note 4: Cash and other monetary assets

CFPB has both cash and investments held outside of Treasury. When transfers are made from the Board of Governors to CFPB, the funds are deposited into an account held within the FRBNY referred to as the Bureau Fund. The account has a required minimum balance of $250,000 and any funds in excess of this minimum are invested in Treasury securities in increments of $100,000 by the FRBNY utilizing an automatic investment process based on direction from CFPB. CFPB requests cash disbursement from the Bureau Fund to the CFPB's Fund Balance with Treasury based on projections of future cash outlays.

Funds obtained by, transferred to, or credited to the Bureau Fund are immediately available to CFPB and under the control of the Director, and shall remain available until expended, to pay for the expenses of the Bureau in carrying out its duties and responsibilities. Any civil penalty obtained from any person in any judicial or administrative action under Federal consumer financial laws is deposited into the Civil Penalty Fund. Amounts in the Civil Penalty Fund are immediately available to CFPB and under the control of the Director, and shall remain available until expended, for payments to victims of activities for which civil penalties have been imposed. To the extent that such victims cannot be located or such payments are otherwise not practicable, the Bureau may use funds in the Civil Penalty Fund for the purpose of consumer education and financial literacy programs.

In enforcement actions and proceedings under Federal consumer financial laws, a court or the CFPB may order any appropriate legal or equitable relief for a violation of Federal consumer financial law. Relief provided may include certain types of monetary relief, including refunds, restitution, disgorgement, and civil penalties. The CFPB deposits civil penalties it obtains in these judicial and administrative actions into the Civil Penalty Fund. The CFPB makes biannual allocations from the Civil Penalty Fund. As of September 30, 2014, the cash balance in the Civil Penalty Fund was $157 million. During FY 2014 and FY 2013, the CFPB had allocated a total of $31.3 million in compensable harm to victims, $13.4 million for consumer education and financial literacy programs, and $1.6 million in administrative costs. Victim compensationof $30.3 million (net of $ 1 million of distributions in FY 2014) is reported as a liability and displayed as "Civil Penalty Fund Allocation" on the balance sheet as of September 30, 2014. No distributions were made from the Civil Penalty Fund in FY 2013.

Funds obtained by or transferred to the Bureau Fund shall not be construed to be Government funds or appropriated monies. Funds in the Bureau Fund and the Civil Penalty Fund are not subject to apportionment for purposes of chapter 15 Title 31, United States Code, or under any other authority.

Account balances as of September 30, 2014 and September 30, 2013:

	2014	2013
Cash		
Cash Held in the Bureau Fund at the Federal Reserve	265,163	325,312
Cash Held in the Civil Penalty Fund at the Federal Reserve	157,001,716	81,520,001
Total Cash and Other Monetary Assets	$ 157,266,879	$ 81,845,313

Note 5: Accounts receivable

Accounts receivable represents amounts owed to the CFPB by the Public. Account balances as of September 30, 2014 and September 30, 2013:

	2014		2013	
Accounts Receivable:				
Bureau Fund	$	155,575	$	45,692
Civil Penalty Fund		15,200,000		-
Custodial Funds		7,807		9,191
Total Accounts Receivable	$	15,363,382	$	54,883

Note 6: Property, equipment and software, net

Schedule of Property, Equipment, and Software as of September 30, 2014 consist of the following:

Major Class	Acquisition Cost	Accumulated Amortization/Depreciation		Net Book Value
Furniture & Equipment	$15,432,387	$	3,971,039	$11,461,348
Internal Use Software	17,226,280		4,823,716	12,402,564
Leasehold (Capital) Improvement-in-Development	9,561,227		N/A	9,561,227
Software-in-Development	4,071,459		N/A	4,071,459
Total	$46,291,353	$	8,794,755	$37,496,598

Schedule of Property, Equipment, and Software as of September 30, 2013 consist of the following:

Major Class	Acquisition Cost	Accumulated Amortization/Depreciation		Net Book Value
Furniture & Equipment	$ 8,320,022	$	2,485,208	$ 5,834,814
Internal Use Software	12,576,978		1,834,265	10,742,713
Leasehold (Capital) Improvement-in-Development	6,075,513		N/A	6,075,513
Software-in-Development	5,031,437		N/A	5,031,437
Total	$32,003,950	$	4,319,473	$27,684,477

Note 7: Advances & prepayments

Advances and Prepayment balances as of September 30, 2014 and September 30, 2013 were as follows:

	2014	2013
Intragovernmental		
Advances and Prepayments	$ 2,900,006	$ 4,993,642
Total Intragovernmental Other Assets	$ 2,900,006	$ 4,993,642
With the Public		
Advances and Prepayments	$ 2,706	$ 749,699
Total Public Other Assets	$ 2,706	$ 749,699

The intragovernmental advance and prepayment balance is primarily comprised of $1.9 million for FY 2014 represents prepayments made to the Board of Governors for the Office of Inspector General services on a calendar year basis and represents funds needed for the period October 1 through December 31, 2014. The intragovernmental advance balance of $5 million for FY 2013 represents funds advanced and prepaid to the Department of the Treasury for services provided by the working capital fund and funds advanced to FHFA for the development & maintenance of a joint National Mortgage Database. Other advances and prepayments include subscriptions and other miscellaneous items.

Note 8: Other liabilities

Other liabilities as of September 30, 2014 and September 30, 2013 consist of the following:

	2014		2013
Intragovernmental Liabilities			
FECA Liability	$ 162,816	$	46,110
Payroll Taxes Payable	271,377		215,510
Custodial Liability	7,807		9,191
Total Intragovernmental Liabilities	$ 442,000	$	270,811
With the Public			
Employee Withholdings	$ 14,171	$	864
Other	1		-
Total Public Liabilities	$ 14,172	$	864

All other liabilities are considered current liabilities.

Note 9: Liabilities not covered by budgetary resources

Liabilities not covered by budgetary resources as of September 30, 2014 and September 30, 2013 consist of the following:

	2014		2013
Intragovernmental			
FECA	$ 162,816	$	46,110
Benefits Payable	11,669,945		6,097,058
With the Public			
Unfunded Leave	16,400,954		11,939,809
Actuarial FECA	1,179,641		-
Total Liabilities Not Covered by Budgetary Resources	$ 29,413,356	$	18,082,977
Total Liabilities Covered by Budgetary Resources	120,007,024		60,496,884
Total Liabilities	$ 149,420,380	$	78,579,861

As described in Note 1.O., other liabilities include costs for post-retirement benefits for CFPB employees retiring under the Federal Reserve retirement plans.

Note 10: Commitments and contingencies

CFPB is responsible for reimbursing the Federal Reserve Retirement Plan for certain costs related to employees, transferred to CFPB under Section 1064 of the Dodd Frank Act, that enroll in the Plan. A memorandum of understanding between the Board of Governors and the Bureau established that the Board of Governors would provide the Bureau a final cost estimate for this payment by September 30, 2014. CFPB has not yet received that estimate as of November 10, 2014.

The Civil Penalty Fund Administrator made the third allocation from the Civil Penalty Fund on May 30, 2014. At that time, the Fund Administrator determined that there were five cases with classes of victims who are eligible for payment from the Civil Penalty Fund but whose uncompensated harm cannot be estimated at this time. The Fund Administrator will make the fourth allocation from the Civil Penalty Fund on November 29, 2014. At that time, there will be 18 cases considered for allocation and the total amount available for allocation is $112.8 million. As of September 30, 2014, no amounts were accrued in the financial statements for these cases as the future outflows of resources do not meet the definition of probable and estimable.

Note 11: Intragovernmental costs and exchange revenue

Intragovernmental costs represent goods and services provided between two reporting entities within the Federal government, and are in contrast to those with non-federal entities (the public). Earned exchanged revenue with the public results from transactions between the Federal government and a non-Federal entity.

Such costs and earned revenues for fiscal years 2014 and 2013 are summarized as follows:

	2014	2013
Prevent Financial Harm to Consumers While Promoting Good Practices That Benefit Them		
Intragovernmental Costs	$ 55,377,866	$ 35,736,563
Public Costs	173,000,661	130,384,278
Total Program Costs	228,378,527	166,120,841
Net Prevent Financial Harm to Consumers While Promoting Good Practices That Benefit Them Cost	$ 228,378,527	$ 166,120,841
Empower Consumers to Live Better Financial Lives		
Intragovernmental Costs	$ 24,422,060	$ 15,256,926
Public Costs	76,294,606	55,664,649
Total Program Costs	100,716,666	70,921,575
Net Empower Consumers to Live Better Financial Lives Cost	$ 100,716,666	$ 70,921,575
Inform The Public, Policy Makers, and the CFPB's own Policy-Making with Data-Driven Analysis of Consumer Finance Markets and Consumer Behavior		
Intragovernmental Costs	$ 11,096,950	$ 9,281,517
Public Costs	34,666,914	33,863,466
Total Program Costs	45,763,864	43,144,983
Less: Public Earned Revenue	(80,000)	-
Net Inform The Public, Policy Makers, and the CFPB's own Policy-Making with Data-Driven Analysis of Consumer Finance Markets and Consumer Behavior Cost	$ 45,683,864	$ 43,144,983
Advance the CFPB's Performance by Maximizing Resource Productivity & Enhancing Impact		
Intragovernmental Costs	$ 25,861,445	$ 23,908,320
Public Costs	96,913,246	87,229,123
Total Program Costs	122,774,691	111,137,443
Net Advance the CFPB's Performance by Maximizing Resource Productivity & Enhancing Impact Cost	$ 122,774,691	$ 111,137,443
Total Intragovernmental Costs	$ 116,758,321	$ 84,183,326
Total Public Costs	380,875,427	307,141,516
Total Program Costs	497,633,748	391,324,842
Less: Total Public Earned Revenue	(80,000)	-
Total Program Net Cost	$ 497,553,748	$ 391,324,842

Note 12: Apportionment categories of obligations incurred

All obligations incurred are characterized as Category E, Exempt from apportionment (i.e., not apportioned), on the Statement of Budgetary Resources. Obligations incurred and reported in the Statement of Budgetary Resources in fiscal years 2014 and 2013 consisted of the following:

	2014	2013
Direct Obligations, Category E	$ 499,732,046	$ 538,759,116
Reimbursable Obligations, Category E	80,000	-
Total Obligations Incurred	$ 499,812,046	$ 538,759,116

Note 13: Undelivered orders at the end of the period

SFFAS 7, *Accounting for Revenue and Other Financing Sources and Concepts for Reconciling Budgetary and Financial Accounting*, states that the amount of budgetary resources obligated for undelivered orders at the end of the period should be disclosed. CFPB's Undelivered Orders represent obligated amounts designated for future payment of goods and services ordered but not received.

Undelivered Orders as of September 30, 2014 and September 30, 2013 were as follows:

	2014	2013
Total Undelivered Orders at the End of the Period	$ 245,130,881	$ 235,009,127

Note 14: Reconciliation of net cost to budget

CFPB has reconciled its budgetary obligations and non-budgetary resources available to its net cost of operations for the periods ended September 30, 2014 and September 30, 2013.

CONSUMER FINANCIAL PROTECTION BUREAU
RECONCILIATION OF NET COST OF OPERATIONS TO BUDGET
For the Fiscal Years Ended September 30, 2014 and 2013
(In Dollars)

	2014	2013
Resources Used to Finance Activities:		
Budgetary Resources Obligated		
Obligations Incurred	$ 499,812,046	$ 538,759,116
Less: Spending Authority From Offsetting Collections and Recoveries	(15,192,045)	(8,834,619)
Net Obligations	484,620,001	529,924,497
Other Resources		
Imputed Financing From Costs Absorbed By Others	1,517,498	1,848,849
Total Resources Used to Finance Activities	486,137,499	531,773,346
Resources Used to Finance Items Not Part of the Net Cost of Operations:		
Change In Budgetary Resources Obligated For Goods,		
Services and Benefits Ordered But Not Yet Provided	(7,281,125)	(139,842,104)
Resources That Finance the Acquisition of Assets	(13,536,261)	(24,335,242)
Total Resources Used to Finance Items Not Part of Net Cost of Operations	(20,817,386)	(164,177,346)
Total Resources Used to Finance the Net Cost of Operations	465,320,113	367,596,000
Components of the Net Cost of Operations That Will Not Require or		
Generate Resources in the Current Period:		
Components Requiring or Generating Resources in Future Periods		
Increase In Annual Leave Liability	4,461,145	4,172,585
Civil Penalty Fund Allocation	17,288,556	13,046,046
Increase In Post Retirement Health Benefits	5,572,887	4,020,389
Other	1,296,347	45,690
Total Components of Net Cost of Operations That Will Require or		
Generate Resources In Future Periods	28,618,935	21,284,710
Components Not Requiring or Generating Resources		
Depreciation and Amortization	4,475,283	2,470,726
Revaluation of Assets or Liabilities	(751,143)	-
Other	(109,440)	(26,594)
Total Components of Net Cost of Operations That Will Not Require or		
Generate Resources	3,614,700	2,444,132
Total Components of Net Cost of Operations That Will Not Require or		
Generate Resources In The Current Period	32,233,635	23,728,842
Net Cost of Operations	$ 497,553,748	$ 391,324,842

Note 15: President's Budget

Statement of Federal Financial Accounting Standards 7, *Accounting for Revenue and Other Financing Sources and Concepts for Reconciling Budgetary and Financial Accounting*, requires explanations of material differences between amounts reported in the Statement of Budgetary Resources and the actual balances published in the Budget of the United States Government (President's Budget). However, the President's Budget that will include fiscal year 2014 actual budgetary execution information has not yet been published. The President's Budget is scheduled for publication in February 2015 and can be found at the OMB Web site: *http://www.whitehouse.gov/omb/*. The 2015 Budget of the United States Government, with the "Actual" column completed for 2013, has been reconciled to the 2013 Statement of Budgetary Resources and there were no material differences.

	Budgetary Resources	Obligations Incurred	Net Outlays
Combined Statement of Budgetary Resources	$ 708,690,708	$ 538,759,116	$ 356,506,853
Rounding	309,292	240,884	493,147
Budget of U.S. Government	709,000,000	539,000,000	357,000,000
Total Unreconciled Difference	$ -	$ -	$ -

Note 16: Rental payments for space

For all Interagency Agreements the CFPB enters into with another Federal Agency, the CFPB records the rental payments based on the stated monthly amount due in the occupancy agreement.

DESCRIPTION OF AGREEMENT

A. Interagency agreement with the Department of the Treasury's Office of the Comptroller of the Currency (OCC) for space to accommodate the CFPB staff assigned to its headquarters in Washington, DC. The occupancy agreement with OCC covers use of the premises for a period of 20 years expiring on February 17, 2032 with two optional five (5) year renewal periods expiring February 17, 2037 and 2042 respectively. The annual rent shall escalate two percent each year.

Future Payments Due:

Fiscal Year	Buildings
2015	$ 11,822,235
2016	12,061,452
2017	12,305,453
2018	12,554,334
2019	12,808,193
2020 through February 17, 2032	181,758,396
Total Future Payments	$243,310,063

DESCRIPTION OF AGREEMENT

B. Occupancy Agreement (OA) between the CFPB and the General Services Administration for supplies, services and the use of space at 1275 First Street, N.E., Washington D.C. The OA is for a period of 18 months expiring October 31, 2015. The rent is to be adjusted annually for operating cost and real estate taxes. The CFPB entered into this OA in order to secure temporary swing space while the CFPB undergoes a full-building renovation of its primary headquarters located at 1700 G Street, NW, Washington DC. The space assigned in this OA will permit the CFPB to conduct a single-phase renovation. Upon completion of the renovation, the CFPB plans to vacate the space governed by this OA and return to its primary headquarters.

Future Payments Due:

Fiscal Year	Buildings
2015	10,700,287
2016 through October 31, 2015	2,413,492
Total Future Payments	$ 13,113,779

DESCRIPTION OF AGREEMENT

C. Interagency agreement with the Federal Housing Finance Agency (FHFA) for supplies, services and the use of space at 1625 I Street, N.W., Washington D.C. The interagency agreement is for 3 years and 3 months expiring on June 30, 2015. The annual rent shall escalate four percent each year.

Future Payments Due:

Fiscal Year	Buildings
2015 through June 30, 2015	2,318,608
Total Future Payments	$ 2,318,608

DESCRIPTION OF AGREEMENT

D. Occupancy Agreement (OA) between the CFPB and the General Services Administration for supplies, services and the use of space at 140 East 45th Street, New York, NY. The OA is for a period of 120 months expiring September 28, 2023. The rent is to be adjusted annually for operating cost and real estate taxes.

Future Payments Due:

Fiscal Year	Buildings
2015	1,120,401
2016	1,129,645
2017	1,139,166
2018	1,148,974
2019	1,261,041
2020 to September 28, 2023	5,151,376
Total Future Payments	$ 10,950,603

DESCRIPTION OF AGREEMENT

E. Occupancy Agreement (OA) between the CFPB and the General Services Administration for supplies, services and the use of space at 301 Howard Street, San Francisco, California. The OA is for a period of 54 months expiring December 16, 2017. The rent is to be adjusted annually for operating cost and real estate taxes.

Future Payments Due:

Fiscal Year	Buildings
2015	934,515
2016	1,003,488
2017	1,026,498
2018	257,577
Total Future Payments	$ 3,222,078

DESCRIPTION OF AGREEMENT

F. Occupancy Agreement (OA) between the CFPB and the General Services Administration for supplies, services and the use of space at 230 S. Dearborn Street, Chicago, IL. The OA is for a period of 60 months expiring June 30, 2019. The rent is to be adjusted annually for operating cost.

Future Payments Due:

Fiscal Year	Buildings
2015	$ 486,207
2016	488,293
2017	490,423
2018	492,598
2019 through June 30, 2019	370,740
Total Future Payments	$ 2,328,261

DESCRIPTION OF AGREEMENT

G. Occupancy Agreement (OA) between the CFPB and the General Services Administration for supplies, services and the use of space at 1800 F Street N.W., Washington D.C. The OA is for a period of 34 months expiring August 15, 2017. The rent is to be adjusted annually for operating cost. The CFPB entered into this OA in order to secure temporary swing space while the CFPB undergoes a full-building renovation of its primary headquarters located at 1700 G Street, NW, Washington DC. The space assigned in this OA will permit the CFPB to continue to provide space for the Small Savers Childcare Development Center.

Future Payments Due:

Future Payments Due:

Fiscal Year	Buildings
2015	$ 325,839
2016	$ 357,102
2017 through August 15, 2017	$ 328,988
Total Future Payments	$ 1,011,929

Note 17: Funds from dedicated collections

Provided below is summary consolidated component entity information for CFPB's two primary funds from dedicated collections -- the Bureau Fund and the Civil Penalty Fund. Custodial collections (disgorgement paid and FOIA fees collected) reside in non-budgetary FBWT accounts and are excluded from this presentation.

	Bureau Fund	Civil Penalty Fund	FY 2014

A. Fund Balances & Status of Funds:

Fund Balances:

	Bureau Fund	Civil Penalty Fund	FY 2014
Special Fund	$ 38,961,246	$ 696,964	$ 39,658,210
Total	$ 38,961,246	$ 696,964	$ 39,658,210

Status of Fund Balance with Treasury:

Unobligated Balance

	Bureau Fund	Civil Penalty Fund	FY 2014
Available	$ 139,827,331	$ 157,079,108	$ 296,906,439
Obligated Balance Not Yet Disbursed	334,175,480	619,572	$ 334,795,052
Investments at Cost	(434,776,402)	-	(434,776,402)
Cash Held Outside of Treasury	(265,163)	(157,001,716)	(157,266,879)
Total	$ 38,961,246	$ 696,964	$ 39,658,210

B. Summary Assets, Liabilities, and Net Position:

Assets:

	Bureau Fund	Civil Penalty Fund	FY 2014
Total Intragovernmental	$ 476,654,725	$ 696,964	$ 477,351,689
Cash and Other Monetary Assets	265,163	157,001,716	157,266,879
Other	37,662,686	15,200,000	52,862,686
Total Summary Assets	$ 514,582,574	$ 172,898,680	$ 687,481,254

Liabilities and Net Position:

	Bureau Fund	Civil Penalty Fund	FY 2014
Total Liabilities	$ 119,058,422	$ 30,361,958	149,420,380
Cumulative Results of Operations	395,524,152	142,536,722	538,060,874
Total Liabilities & Net Position	$ 514,582,574	$ 172,898,680	$ 687,481,254

C. Summary Statement of Net Cost:

	Bureau Fund	Civil Penalty Fund	FY 2014
Total Gross Program Costs	$ 478,994,514	$ 18,639,234	497,633,748
Less: Total Earned Revenues	(80,000)		(80,000)
Net Cost of Operations	$ 478,914,514	$ 18,639,234	$ 497,553,748

D. Summary Statement of Changes in Net Position:

	Bureau Fund	Civil Penalty Fund	FY 2014
Net Position Beginning of Period	$ 338,835,330	$ 68,473,955	$ 407,309,285
Total Financing Sources	535,603,336	92,702,001	628,305,337
Net Cost of Operations	(478,914,514)	(18,639,234)	(497,553,748)
Change in Net Position	56,688,822	74,062,767	130,751,589
Net Position End of Period	$ 395,524,152	$ 142,536,722	$ 538,060,874

	Bureau Fund	Civil Penalty Fund	FY 2013
A. Fund Balances & Status of Funds:			
Fund Balances:			
Special Fund	$ 26,764,046	$ -	$ 26,764,046
Total	$ 26,764,046	$ -	$ 26,764,046
Status of Fund Balance with Treasury:			
Unobligated Balance			
Available	$ 88,437,750	$ 81,493,842	$ 169,931,592
Obligated Balance Not Yet Disbursed	282,424,613	26,159	282,450,772
Investments at Cost	(343,773,005)	-	(343,773,005)
Cash Held Outside of Treasury	(325,312)	(81,520,001)	(81,845,313)
Total	$ 26,764,046	$ -	$ 26,764,046
B. Summary Assets, Liabilities, and Net Position:			
Assets:			
Total Intragovernmental	$ 375,554,774	$ -	$ 375,554,774
Cash and Other Monetary Assets	325,312	81,520,001	81,845,313
Other	28,489,059	-	28,489,059
Total Summary Assets	$ 404,369,145	$ 81,520,001	$ 485,889,146
Liabilities and Net Position:			
Total Liabilities	$ 65,533,815	$ 13,046,046	$ 78,579,861
Cumulative Results of Operations	338,835,330	68,473,955	407,309,285
Total Liabilities & Net Position	$ 404,369,145	$ 81,520,001	$ 485,889,146
C. Summary Statement of Net Cost:			
Total Gross Program Costs	$ 378,278,796	$ 13,046,046	$ 391,324,842
Net Cost of Operations	$ 378,278,796	$ 13,046,046	$ 391,324,842
D. Summary Statement of Changes in Net Position:			
Net Position Beginning of Period	$ 196,503,943	$ 32,000,000	$ 228,503,943
Total Financing Sources	520,610,183	49,520,001	570,130,184
Net Cost of Operations	(378,278,796)	(13,046,046)	(391,324,842)
Change in Net Position	142,331,387	36,473,955	178,805,342
Net Position End of Period	$ 338,835,330	$ 68,473,955	$ 407,309,285

Note 18: Subsequent events

Since October 2014, the CFPB has entered into one Consent Order with an entity for violations of Federal consumer financial law. The Order required the entity to pay in $200,000 in civil monetary penalties to the CFPB's Civil Penalty Fund. The Order was agreed to, and the amount ordered was paid in fiscal year 2015. Further, CFPB collected accounts receivable from fiscal year 2014 imposed penalties of $15.2 million and Bureau Administer Redress of $27.5 million.

In October 2014, the Bureau and an entity which violated Federal consumer financial law entered into an agreement requiring the entity to disgorge funds to Treasury. That agreement will result in the disgorgement of $6.8 million in fiscal year 2015.

A Civil Penalty Fund distribution also occurred in fiscal year 2015. In the National Legal Help Center case $1.2 million was distributed to harmed consumers.

Note 19: Fiduciary activities

Section 1055 of the Dodd-Frank Act authorizes the court in a judicial action, or the CFPB in an administrative proceeding, to grant any appropriate legal or equitable relief for a violation of Federal consumer financial law. Such relief may include redress for victims of the violations, including refunds, restitution, and damages. Funds paid as relief that is intended to compensate victims of violations are treated as fiduciary funds and deposited into the "Legal or Equitable Relief Fund" established at the Department of the Treasury. Fiduciary assets are not assets of the CFPB. The victims have an ownership interest in the cash or other assets held by the CFPB under provision of law, regulation, or other fiduciary arrangement

During fiscal years 2014 and 2013, the CFPB had the following fiduciary activity:

CONSUMER FINANCIAL PROTECTION BUREAU
SCHEDULE OF FIDUCIARY ACTIVITY
For the Year Ended September 30, 2013 and 2012
(In Dollars)

	2014		2013
	Consumer Financial Legal or Equitable Relief Fund		
Fiduciary Net Assets, Beginning of Year	$ 122,804	$	-
Fiduciary Revenues Collected	28,231,130		122,804
Fiduciary Revenues Receivables	29,599,000		-
Administrative Expenses	(23,146)		-
Disbursements to and on behalf of beneficiaries	(9,311,987)		-
Increase/(Decrease) in Fiduciary Net Assets	48,494,997		122,804
Fiduciary Net Assets, End of Year	$ 48,617,801	$	122,804

CONSUMER FINANCIAL PROTECTION BUREAU
SCHEDULE OF FIDUCIARY ACTIVITY
As of September 30, 2014 and 2013
(In Dollars)

	2014		2013
	Consumer Financial Legal or Equitable Relief Fund		
Fiduciary Assets:			
Cash	$ 19,019,186	$	122,804
Accounts Receivable	29,599,000		-
Fiduciary Liabilities:			
Less: Liabilities	385		-
Total Fiduciary Net Assets	$ 48,617,801	$	122,804

2.3 Other information

The following Schedule of Spending presents an overview of the funds available for the CFPB to spend and how the CFPB spent these funds as of and for the fiscal year ended September 30, 2014. The financial data used to populate this schedule is the same underlying data used to populate the CFPB's Statement of Budgetary Resources. Similar data can be found on www.USAspending.gov for goods and services purchased via contracts with non-Federal vendors.

CONSUMER FINANCIAL PROTECTION BUREAU
OTHER ACCOMPANING INFORMATION
SCHEDULE OF SPENDING
For The Periods Ended September 30, 2014 and 2013
(In Dollars)

	2014	2013
What Money is Available to Spend?		
Total Resources	$ 796,718,485	$ 708,690,708
Less Amount Not Agreed to be Spent	(296,906,439)	(169,931,592)
Total Amounts Agreed to be Spent	$ 499,812,046	$ 538,759,116
How was the Money Spent?		
Personnel Compensation	$ 171,702,260	$ 143,341,164
Personnel Benefits	65,271,703	48,998,214
Benefits for Former Personnel	39,246	70,856
Travel and transportation of persons	17,232,663	14,484,205
Transportation of things	114,159	154,148
Rent, Communications, and utilities	11,049,627	5,611,501
Printing and reproduction	2,424,626	2,227,636
Other contractual services	201,948,343	136,816,460
Supplies and materials	4,552,106	4,659,969
Equipment	21,452,780	31,586,601
Land and structures	4,023,950	150,805,839
Interest and dividends	211	2,523
Other	372	-
Total Spending	499,812,046	538,759,116
Total Amounts Agreed to be Spent	$ 499,812,046	$ 538,759,116
Who did the Money go to?		
Federal	$ 131,721,047	$ 237,635,415
Non-Federal	368,090,999	301,123,701
Total Amounts Agreed to be Spent	$ 499,812,046	$ 538,759,116

The presentation for the fiscal year 2013 column was reclassified and now reflects the amounts consistent with the required reporting for fiscal year 2014 column, per OMB Circular A-136 issued in September 2014. The difference in reporting is spending by categories on an obligation incurred basis rather than a disbursement basis.